Praise for *History of a Suicide*

"Elegiac. . . . Affecting. . . . Bialosky's detective work becomes a form of mourning, and a means of getting past it."

— The New Yorker

"Bialosky's language is plain but enveloping. . . . Her hand is always skillful, as attentive to the rhythms of storytelling as to conveying emotion."

— Time

"Valiant and eloquent. . . . Bialosky's thoughtful book elucidates the complexity of suicide."

— The Washington Post Book World

"A profound and lyrical investigation. . . . Bialosky writes sensitively and beautifully."

— New York

"Moments of exquisite pain and surprising joy."
— O, The Oprah Magazine (Top 10 Titles to Pick Up Now)

"Poignant and resonant."

— The Cleveland Plain Dealer

"Brave and beautifully crafted."

— The Daily Beast

"Quietly piercing."

— Library Journal

"An extraordinarily valiant and resonant testimony to the healing powers of truth and empathy."

— Booklist

"The plain language of Bialosky's title reflects this book's quiet, intimate and profoundly understated art: a clear medium penetrating into the wounded and wounding mystery of her subject."

—Robert Pinsky, former United States Poet Laureate

"That rare book that is so articulate and stunningly close to the bone that one holds one's breath while reading it."

—A. M. Homes, author of
This Book Will Save Your Life

"Beautiful and incredibly brave. . . . Jill Bialosky has stared straight into the white hot heart of something very-nearly unspeakable."

—Dani Shapiro, author of *Devotion*

"An extraordinary book . . . [that] also serves as a practical road map to understanding why life can become unbearable for someone who seems extravagantly gifted."

—Susan Cheever, author of *Home Before Dark*

"Jill Bialosky is such a fearless and clear-eyed and compassionate writer that although we know from the start how the story she tells will turn out, we cannot stop reading."

—George Howe Colt, author of *November of the Soul*

"Like a match in the darkness, Jill Bialosky's stirring memoir sheds light on a fathomless mystery."

—Melanie Thernstrom, author of *The Pain Chronicles*

"Could things have been different? That is the inevitable, haunting question after a suicide. It can never be answered, only explored; and Jill Bialosky explores it with intelligence, integrity, a poet's sensitivity, and a sister's enduring love."

—Joan Wickersham, author of *The Suicide Index*

"Bialosky writes about despair with such elegance and perspicacity that the reader, paradoxically, is returned to hope, page after gleaming page."

Lauren Slater, author of *Prozac Diary*

"*History of a Suicide* is an important contribution to literature. More than that, it is a gift overflowing with compassion."

—Beth Kephart, National Book Award finalist and author of *You Are My Only* on her blog

"A gorgeous and haunting portrait of grief and the particular hauntedness of those left reeling in the wake of a suicide. Some kinds of loss can only be named by lyric means and a poet's memoir is the perfect form to take on this hefty and courageous task. It'll be with me for a long time."

—Melissa Febos, author of the national bestseller *Girlhood* also by jill bialosky

Asylum

Poetry Will Save Your Life

The Prize

The Players

Intruder

The Life Room

House under Snow

Subterranean

Wanting a Child
(co-edited with Helen Schulman)

The End of Desire

HISTORY OF A SUICIDE

my sister's unfinished life

JILL BIALOSKY

WASHINGTON
SQUARE PRESS

ATRIA

new york   london   toronto   sydney   new delhi

WASHINGTON SQUARE PRESS

ATRIA

An Imprint of Simon & Schuster, Inc.
1230 Avenue of the Americas
New York, NY 10020

This Atria/Washington Square Press trade paperback edition November 2022

WASHINGTON SQUARE PRESS / ATRIA PAPERBACK and colophon
are registered trademarks of Simon & Schuster, Inc.

For information about special discounts for bulk purchases,
please contact Simon & Schuster Special Sales at
1-866-506-1949 or business@simonandschuster.com.

The Simon & Schuster Speakers Bureau can bring authors
to your live event. For more information or to book an event
contact the Simon & Schuster Speakers Bureau at
1-866-248-3049 or visit our website at www.simonspeakers.com.

Designed by Suet Yee Chong

Manufactured in the United States of America

3 5 7 9 10 8 6 4 2

The Library of Congress has cataloged the hardcover edition as follows:

Bialosky, Jill.
History of a Suicide : my sister's unfinished life / Jill Bialosky.
p. cm.
1. Suicide. 2. Suicide victims—Family relationships.
3. Bereavement—Psychological aspects. I. Title.
HV6545.B476 2011
362.28092—dc22
[B]
2010047134

ISBN 978-1-4391-0193-3
ISBN 978-1-4391-0194-0 (pbk)
ISBN 978-1-4391-3474-0 (ebook)

for kim
july 19, 1968–april 16, 1990

A Sister's Story

My sister startles herself from sleep.
I can feel her breath rise
in the slow-motion of mine.
I am thirteen, and she is three.

Outside sleep unravels from our bodies.
Her hand, perfect for cradling a coin,
closes within mine.
We walk in the backyard

over long grass,
between weeping willow trees.
She won't remember her dream
so I tell her another;

how a girl alone in the night,
the stars so close to her,
she takes a pair of scissors
and cuts them from the sky.

She opens her slate-colored book,
arranges the stars
into constellations,
pastes them flat as doilies.

They are like a billion
burning hearts.
Each morning the book
stretches back to the sky.

JILL BIALOSKY

in memory of kim

andrew solomon

There is a statistic, much bandied around in psychiatric circles, that every suicide affects 135 people. It's a good statistic to bear in mind when trying to understand the phenomenon of self-annihilation, especially because suicidal people often believe that their departure from the world will hardly be noticed. But it is also a peculiar average; some people's suicides presumably affect far fewer people than that and some far more. Even that, however, is in many ways a meaningless sentence, because it presumes some sharp delineation between the affected and the unaffected, when in reality there is only the progression from deeply affected to less deeply affected to slightly affected to unaffected. I have been intimately affected by the suicide of my college roommate, who was a beloved friend, and by one of my son's classmates; I have likewise been affected by suicides I've read about here or there, by the suicide of my parents' friends' son, by what I think was the suicide of the daughter of professional acquaintances. We are all affected by the constant affirmation that suicide is a possibility for people we love and for us, a truth made evident by every suicide we hear about. The suicide of a distant antecedent one never met lives on in family lore and makes the act feel more accessible. So, 135 people? The yen for precision is almost touching.

Most of those who die by suicide are eulogized by intimates, to live on in the oral tradition of a given family and its penumbra of friends. It is hard to speak of luck in relation to suicide, but there is some poetic justice in the striving after knowledge—of the person who has died, of the self, of the larger society—that can ensue. In sharing her quest to make logic, if not sense, of her sister's death, Jill Bialosky has ensured that Kim's perishing affected not 135 people, but the thousands who have had the good fortune to read *History of a Suicide*. This is, above all, a book about Kim and a solid piece of evidence that she was loved well and constantly. Like all suicide memoirs, it is a plea for forgiveness, an unsteady investigation into whether there was anything the author could have done that would have changed the outcome. It is a journey into the nightmare of a mind in decay.

Jill Bialosky writes with lyrical precision in the well-honed voice of a poet, but where one might hope for great truths, she narrates bewilderment. The reality is that suicide is incomprehensible except to the people who attempt or complete it—and often, even to them. Kim had been cruelly rejected by a cold-hearted father and it is clear that there was no recovery from that injury, which exacerbated her underlying fragility. But Kim was also unknowable; she kept her inner life from her mother and her sisters, and her dying made evident a relentless suffering that languished in obscurity before the night she went to the garage and asphyxiated herself. This book is a tribute to Kim; it is also an exercise in self-reproach, an expression of Bialosky's sadness at not having understood the depth of Kim's despair before her desperate act. Bravely, Bialosky also evinces some of the anger that every suicide engenders — anger at both herself and Kim. In her pondering of the nature of suicide, she looks to vitality and ponders how readers might know either Kim's despair or Bialosky's own bereavement; this book is as much a cautionary tale as an attempt to redeem some of the beauty of Kim's life. Bialosky wants a memorial to her sister; she also wants to express her grief by spreading it among the anonymous voyeurs who immerse themselves in these pages.

It's hard to grow attached to Kim as she is set forth here; she held back too much, made too many unnecessary mistakes, resisted help that was amply offered. But it is easy to grow attached to Bialosky's deep longing for her sister. Bialosky gives us the person she knew, but seldom wavers from the realization that Kim was also someone else, someone she didn't know and for whom she has been searching ever since the suicide. Bialosky finds Kim's abandoning father as agonizingly inaccessible as Kim herself, and is equally unsettled by a boyfriend who never quite comes into focus, a boyfriend Bialosky could not imagine loving and whom Kim could not imagine leaving. Kim died abruptly, maybe even impulsively, but she also died gradually, withering from the inside out. No one intuited enough to snatch her from her own despair. This is a chronicle of possibilities lost, a narrative of regret that tries but fails to resolve the mystery at its center. It describes the toxic mix of rejection, grief, and dread that corrodes Kim's increasingly futile gestures toward happiness. Kim seems to exist only in relation to other people, and when those people are not with her, her sense of self evaporates, and what seemed to be want blossoms into need.

In some ways, this book is also an anthology: a compendium of fragments from poems, fiction, and essays that inspired or influenced Bialosky, one more elegiac than the next. They reflect the disdain that Kim felt for herself, which is too painful for Bialosky to express without reverting to other writers' language. Kim died a long time ago, but in these pages, she flirts with life again, never fully revealing her psyche despite her flamboyant vulnerability. This book makes you wonder whether you do or can know anyone else; in fact, it proposes that you never do or can. It exposes the stark loneliness of someone who had everything to live for, who was beautiful and beloved but so lost: lost to herself, then lost to her sister, and now, with this book, lost to all of us.

opening words

On a cold day in the autumn of 1998, eight years after my sister died, I went back to Cleveland to visit her grave with my husband, David. It was a bleak, overcast afternoon in November when we drove to the cemetery. My sister Kim is buried in that city of steel skies and flat lands in a place called Mount Olive Cemetery. I like the tone of authority in the name of her burial place. It feels as though she's been anointed, lifted to a place of holiness. The cemetery is on the outskirts of the suburbs. We drove first through the orderly suburban streets, then under a stark bridge that appeared to lead nowhere, and then through the black gates. I thought after all these years that seeing again the sight of her gray headstone and the small plot of land designated to her on this earth would devastate me. Instead a long calm washed through me. I did not cry when I saw Kim's grave. I read the inscription composed by my family: *Kim Elizabeth, July 19, 1968–April 16, 1990, Our Beloved.*

Kim's suicide has forever altered the way in which I respond to the world around me. It has transformed the way I think and feel about intimacy, motherhood, friendship, and our responsibilities to others. Her early death changed every preconceived idea I had of suicide, depression, suffering, parenthood, and our debt to another person. Before Kim ended her life, I thought, like most people, that someone who would take his or her own life was somehow different from the rest of us. I was wrong.

At her gravesite, beneath which lay the box that contained the flesh and bone that had comprised her physical self—the box that eight years earlier I had watched being lowered into the ground and had thrown dirt on top of, a Jewish ritual to signify the family's responsibility to bury their loved ones—I was overcome with a familiar feeling of disbelief. I wanted, like Demeter, goddess of the spring who lost her daughter to the underworld, to plead with the gods to bargain back her life. As the gray afternoon light moved through a stand of trees I wondered, as I had so many times, if Kim had really wanted to die or whether her act had been a cry for help.

I cannot go back to Cleveland without feeling the shadow of Kim over the city. It is in the color of the sky, in the shapes of the familiar houses on our suburban block, in the shade of the bushes along our front walk. Her loss is wrapped inside the tree that shades our yard. When I go into her bedroom—now turned into a kind of den, with a new desk and chair forced awkwardly into the room—I can only see it the way it used to be: Kim's unmade bed, her clothes piled in a corner, her teddy bear thrown on the floor.

I still on occasion wake up in the morning and forget that she is gone, that she'll never be able to have the baby she once wanted, that she'll never know my son. I sometimes catch a quick flash of her face in my mind and it is as if she's looking at me, trying to tell me something. I try very hard to listen.

Kim was the youngest of four girls, the only child of my mother and her second husband, the baby of our family—my baby, I sometimes thought, my Kim. My mother and we three remaining sisters reconstructed the weeks before she died. We read and reread the short suicide note she left. We recounted the last conversations, moods, phone calls; we talked to her friends and boyfriend, hoping that these conversations would explain why she'd left us. Her life and death have shaped each of us in profound ways. We talked and talked, among ourselves, with everyone who knew her, and didn't get far. Then we stopped talking and mourned privately, each in our own way, trying to move on. But I could not really move on. It wasn't until just a few years ago, when my own son—at the cusp of adolescence, soon to be a young man—reached the age at which Kim's life began to falter, that I knew I had to try to understand what happened to my sister. My responsibility as a mother made it imperative. I knew that in order to go on, to live my life, the life I have built with my husband and my son, my life as a writer and an editor, I had to go back and excavate her history. I had to understand why she would take her own life and whether I could have stopped her.

Kim was a decade younger than us, her three older sisters. All of us shared the same biological mother, but Laura, Cindy, and I were born from a different father. Our father came from a family of Jewish immigrants. He died when I was two years old, Laura three, and Cindy nine months. My mother, also Jewish, remarried an Irish Catholic man when I was eight years old; two years later she gave birth to Kim. My mother hoped Kim would bridge our not-yet-sturdy, second, Jewish-Catholic family and restore a home that had been shaped by grief and loss. But three years after Kim was born my mother and stepfather divorced, and our family went back to being a family of women.

When Kim died, I was living in New York City, newly married and three and a half months pregnant with my first child. My older sister, Laura, was also living in New York City, working in an art gallery. Cindy was married and training to be a psychologist in Los Angeles. Kim took her life in my mother's garage, my mother asleep in her upstairs bedroom in the house in Shaker Heights, Ohio, where we had all grown up.

The dialogue we have with the dead is never ending. That day at her grave I told myself that I would write about her for two reasons: to redeem her death, and in so doing honor her, and because I needed to understand what she had done and why in order to move forward with my own life. There were days, weeks, sometimes months when I was engaged with life—with my family, friends, and work—but it was as though Kim's suicide hung over me, at the back of my thoughts, and it would creep up at times and I would feel frightened by it.

If I could recognize the forces that weakened Kim's strength and attempt to re-create her inner world through my writing, perhaps I'd begin to understand what caused her to take her life. And maybe in doing so, I could forgive myself. In her death I was closer to her than I had been the few years before she died when she had kept a wedge between us so I would not catch sight of the troubled person she had become.

How had I let her disappear from view? How had we let her go? These are some of the questions I sought to answer.

Her grave that day seemed lonely amid the graves of strangers. That she was buried alone, not in a family plot (her death was so unexpected that no such arrangements had been made), represented to me the estrangement she had come to feel in life. I took David's arm and listened to the branches creaking overhead. I looked at the gravestones, some covered with fresh-laid flowers, others less attended. On the most fundamental level it did not seem real.

When I was a child, birds in close proximity had frightened me. Their skittish nature reminded me of my own reactions to a world made precarious by the sudden death of my father. But when I saw a school of birds clamber over the sky at Kim's gravesite, making a perfect V in the air, and saw one bird land on one of the monuments near her grave, I was filled with a strange happiness, as if Kim's spirit were alive and present in the opaque November sky. I thought of T. S. Eliot's lines in *Four Quartets:* "Go, go, go, said the bird: / Human kind cannot bear very much reality."

I have twenty-one years of Kim's essence stored up in my memory bank. The fallacy about death is its finality. Kim is as alive for me as if I were still at the foot of her bed, in her childhood room that was once my room, listening to her talk about the pair of jeans she had just bought at the Gap, or the day she had spent at one of the Lake Erie beaches, Mentor-on-the-Lake, with her girlfriends. Or sitting with her around our dining room table, her dirty blond hair fallen over her face as she worked on a thousand-piece puzzle of *Mona Lisa* or Monet's *Yellow Irises with Pink Cloud.*

The gray November sky that afternoon carried within it the truth of something foretold. I regretted again, as I had at her funeral, that we had never given her a proper eulogy—that, too distraught, I had not been able to speak about her and the significance of her young life. Her funeral was shrouded in sorrow, shame, and incredulity. We were struggling to accept that she was gone, no longer able to shake her out of the long drift of delirium that compromised the last years of her life, never to see into her mercurial half-gray, half-blue eyes, never to touch her again. The rabbi spoke for us, said the prayers of mourning into the cold April air as we listened, hoping that the world on the other side of life was a better place. Two days before she killed herself had been my birthday and she had called to wish me a happy day. Happiness no longer seemed part of the equation. The world felt tenuous and unsafe. Then I did not know how to grapple with or incorporate the violence of her act of resignation. I did not know how to grasp that she had wanted, at least that night, to die. Or perhaps had wished in those moments to be unlocked from her pain. It seemed impossible, and I floated in the sea of my disbelief, still thinking that there had been a mistake. Though she was clearly dead—she had to be, my husband picked out her coffin—I could not accept it. I was still worried about her, convinced I could do something to change the course of what had happened. More, I was left with the belief that she had inherited the grief, loneliness, and pain of our family, and that her suicide was partially a result of this burden. I wondered whether Kim's suicide had been inevitable.

Before it happened to Kim, the horror of suicide—that a person could take her life because of searing emotional pain—had seemed, while devastating and tragic, more of an abstract concept. Though I had known a few people who had committed suicide, one a childhood friend, over time I had pushed those losses into my unconscious. For years, even after Kim died, my defenses were formidable. If I were truly to have understood her state of mind then, I would have had to feel her pain unencumbered by the layers of protection I shielded myself with like thick sweaters against the cold. Every time I tried to grasp it I was overcome. It was as if I lived behind a blackened door.

In *Moby-Dick*, Melville's masterpiece, Ishmael tells of his desire to meet the unknown when he undertakes the voyage of the sea in his quest for the whale:

> Why upon your first voyage as a passenger, did you yourself feel such a mystical vibration, when first told that you and your ship were now out of sight of land? Why did the old Persians hold the sea holy? Why did the Greeks give it a separate deity, and make him the own brother of Jove? Surely all this is not without meaning. And still deeper the meaning of that story of Narcissus, who because he could not grasp the tormenting, wild image he saw in the fountain, plunged into it and was drowned. But that same image, we ourselves see in all rivers and oceans. It is the image of the ungraspable phantom of life; and this is the key to it all.

To understand suicide is to try to comprehend the ungraspable phantom of life: the power of the darkness, fear, and weakness within the human mind, a force as mysterious, turbulent, complex, and uncontrollable as the sea, a force so powerful it may not be capable of withstanding its own destructive power. After reading *Moby-Dick*, a treatise on the abyss and the inchoate and terrible power of inner demons, it does not surprise me to learn that Melville's own son Malcolm died of a self-inflicted gunshot wound at the age of eighteen. Perhaps in writing the prophetic, meticulous novel of Ahab's obsessive, diabolical quest for the white whale, Melville had hoped to crack open something of the mystery of his son's or his own despair. Of the need to undertake the voyage, he wrote, "Somehow dreadfully, we are all cracked about the head, and sadly need mending."

The page has been my container, my ship; my words my compass; my memory my harpoon in my desire to wrest coherence from the unwieldy material of personal truth. Whenever I come close to understanding the terrible mystery of suicide, it eludes me again, darting away like the mercurial whale beneath the surface of the ocean, plunging further into the depths of the unknown. When I think I've made my peace with the white beast, it rears its head, continuing to shadow the present. There is a desire to still the chaos, but it catches me when I least expect it.

When a young person ends his or her life, the grief of those left behind is complicated by despair, disbelief, fury, guilt, and shame. But my dismay has never been directed at Kim. It is directed at the world she was born into, the past that shaped what she would have to bear, and the failure of those closest to her and the community around her to offer the support and confidence that might have sustained her. Even in our darkest moments most of us have hope that life will turn for the better. "Hope is the thing with feathers / That perches in the soul," wrote Emily Dickinson. "And sore must be the storm / That could abash the little bird / That kept so many warm."

At Kim's gravesite I told myself that I would try to tell her story. In the years that followed I periodically researched and made notes, but I always put them away again, thwarted by complicated emotions and the moral dilemma of exposing my family's private world, as well as my own.

A few years ago I flew to Los Angeles to spend a few days with Dr. Edwin Shneidman, a leading figure in the study of suicidology. That visit changed the way I thought about suicide, but it wasn't until I began attending a monthly suicide bereavement group and listened to other survivors of suicide tell their stories that I was able, bolstered by the courage of others living with suicide, to write my story, free of disgrace. These pages narrate the story of what happened to Kim and my voyage to come to grips with her suicide. Since I cannot bring her back, I have struggled to make her lapse into darkness and the devastation of suicide understandable. Suicide should never happen to anyone. I want you to know as much as I know. That is the reason I am writing this book.

author's note

Memory is mercurial, granting us access to certain experiences while blocking others from us, as if to protect us from what we cannot face. Writing about Kim has given voice to my memory and its meaning; it has given a shape, however opaque, to her inner world and to my desire to restore grace to her life. It has also given order and context to the experience of living with her memory.

Though in these pages I write about my two other sisters, my mother, and Kim's father, this book is my story of Kim and my interpretation alone of what befell her. I have tried to avoid imposing what others in my family have thought and felt and how Kim's suicide has penetrated their lives. Those stories are their own to tell.

In creating this narrative, along with my own memories and experiences I have quoted from Kim's journals and the personal essays she wrote in school. Those documents have given me access to some of her inner thoughts. I have also reviewed police records, autopsy reports, photos, research about suicide, and works of literature that have helped me paste together what I believe happened to Kim, shedding light on her state of mind. Because literature and poetry often say what we cannot,

I have relied on poets, novelists, and philosophers sometimes for clarity and illumination in these pages, and as a natural extension of my quest to understand.

The italicized sections throughout the text are taken verbatim from Kim's words.

part one

To the person in the bell jar, blank and stopped as
a dead baby, the world itself is the bad dream.

—SYLVIA PLATH, *THE BELL JAR*

WHEN I GO TO SLEEP

These are the bare facts. On the night of April 15, into the early
morning hours of April 16, 1990, Kim went out to a bar in
downtown Cleveland with a few girlfriends. She was fighting
with the boyfriend she had been with since she was seventeen.
In her mind, he had taken on vast importance. She came home—
it must have been after midnight. She parked her car, a blue
Hyundai she had bought with her own money, in the driveway
behind the garage. She was attached to her car. It was the first car
she owned and she was proud that she managed to keep up the
payments from the tips she made waitressing at a delicatessen
called Jack's. My mother was upstairs in her bedroom. I imagine
she was watching television. A chronic insomniac, she used to
watch television until the early hours of the morning.

Kim called her boyfriend shortly after she got home. Her best
friend told me that Kim had learned he was seeing another girl.
Perhaps they fought some more. (Once he'd punched her lights
out and she'd ended up in the hospital. Kim broke up and got

back together with him many times.) She called and told him she was going to a place far away. He told us he thought she was trying to threaten him. He thought, by "far away," that she meant she was leaving Cleveland. Dumb fuck, I wanted to say, after he told us this, when he came to my mother's house dressed uncomfortably in a white-collared shirt and suede blazer to pay his respects. Dark hair pushed back, face white and shattered. I wanted to kick him, but instead, because he was suffering, I opened my arms and hugged him. He took his own life five years later.

Kim must have written the note she left on the kitchen counter, taken my mother's keys from the counter of the built-in bookcases in the living room, left the house, opened the garage door where my mother's white Saab was parked, closed the garage door, and opened the car door. She turned on the ignition and fell asleep inside.

Here is a poem she wrote that was published in the February 1977 issue of the *Sussex Scoop*, her grade-school publication. She was eight years old.

> *When I go to sleep*
> *I kiss my mother*
> *I take my sheep*
> *And tell my brother.*

The cause of death was asphyxiation. The next morning, the young neighborhood boy who mowed my mother's lawn heard the car running, exhaust fumes coming out from beneath the bottom of the garage door. I didn't even know what Kim was wearing. I asked my mother, but no one could remember. My mother was awakened around noon that day by two police officers who broke into the house, came upstairs, and stood in front of her bed. She had taken tranquilizers that night in order to sleep.

Not long before she died, Kim worried about her black and white cat, Gretel, whom she had owned for twelve years and who was very sick. Kim had named her cat after the girl in the fairy tale, the story of the lost girl and boy whose parents abandoned them in the forest and who, afraid they would not find their way back, left a trail of bread crumbs in their wake. Here is a poem Kim wrote about Gretel when she was a child.

My Cat Gretel

Gretel was walking down the walk when
I shouted duck Gretel!. AND HE DID.
The reason I told him to duck was
a mean old man named Mr. Simms was trying
to shoot Gretel. Mr. Simms is 82 years old.
AFTER that I took Gretel to the soda shop
and got him a double catnip soda.
While we were there I told gretel the reason
Mr. Simms tried to shoot him was that Gretel
killed his mouse by mistake. But I do not
blame gretel either. After the soda shop
we went and played going to a dance.
THEN we saw Mr. Simms and he said I am very
sorry Kids Gretel had all ready ran and hid.

I said Gretel you can come out now.
Gretel stayed very close to me he did not trust
Mr. Simms. Just to make sure I said I would
call the police. He walked away.
We went home and ate dinner. I had a bowl of
chicken soap and gretel had some cat nip stew.
Then we went to bed.
The next morning Gretel and me went to school.
On the way home a boy pulled Gretels tail
I siad thats not nice. He siad yes it is.
We ignored him, and went home.

Then we went to bed.

THE END

She had read that when cats die they go off to a secret hiding place and die alone. She thought this was so sad that every time she got home she looked for Gretel, believing that if the cat was in her sight, then she wouldn't die. A month after Kim killed herself, my mother found Gretel curled up dead in the closet in Kim's room.

THE CONTENTS OF HER WALLET

State of Ohio driver's license

Social Security card

Society Super Banking card

Severance's Health Club membership card

Cleveland Heights–University Heights public library card

American Red Cross card (to certify that she had completed the cardiopulmonary resuscitation course)

Vikram Ingrasani, MD, appointment card (a psychiatrist she had seen periodically but was not in direct contact with at the time of her death)

Cuyahoga Community College ID card

Clinique, Higbees Beachwood card

River Oaks Travel business card (was she planning a trip?)

Scandinavian Health & Racket Membership card

May Company credit card

ESC extended service contract for her car

A letter I had written on my office stationery, folded in halves, dated Jan. 20, 1988. I sent her the letter along with a dress I bought for her to wear as my maid of honor at my wedding.

Dear Kim,

Here's the dress in a medium. I hope it fits. If not, send back and I can get you a larger size. I'm also enclosing a book that I edited. I think you'll like it. I'm sorry we didn't have enough time to talk alone in Cleveland. Everything gets so hectic

and then it's time to leave. Any chance of visiting?
Please write to me.

    I love you,

    Jill

In her Statement Savings Bank book the last balance recorded was $182.58. She had made two deposits of forty dollars, one for fifty, and a withdrawal for ten.

FISHBOWL

There is a fishbowl in my kitchen. Inside is a blue Chinese fighting fish my thirteen-year-old son, Lucas, brought home one day from the pet shop. He has owned three fish in his life. I thought we were done with fish but apparently we are not. This time, aware of the short life span of a fish, he prefers to keep the new fish nameless. The first fish he named Clifford. The second was Clifford II. Clifford was black. He swam in the same fishbowl in our kitchen. Lucas, four or five then, fed him flakes of food every day. We helped him clean the fishbowl every week. He liked using the sieve to scoop up the squirming fish, liked watching it flip-flop in the sieve once it was taken out of its element. He liked to go to the pet shop to buy marbles for the bottom of the bowl, then different color coral. He talked to the fish. He ate his bowl of Cheerios at the kitchen counter every morning, and while he fed himself spoonfuls of cereal he watched Clifford swim in his tank and the fish amused him. Perhaps he invented little narrative games

in his mind, the way he did when he played with his action figures. When Clifford died Lucas was in disbelief. It was his first
experience with the death of a living thing, and once we flushed
him down our toilet Lucas was sad. I could tell days later that
when he ate his cereal he still looked at the spot in the kitchen
where we kept Clifford's fishbowl even though the spot was
empty and only the shadow of Clifford remained.

DISBELIEF

We think stupidly that love can be enough. The day of Kim's
funeral was a beautiful April day, the sky cerulean blue and
cloudless. It brought to mind the same unworldly feeling as
the day after the 9/11 attacks on New York City: that the sun
should shine so magnificently seemed audacious amid the tragedy and weight of the occasion.

Everyone close to Kim who gathered under the white canopy at the gravesite must have wondered what he or she might
have said or done that may have affected Kim's act, and our
responsibility left us speechless. An unsettling quiet reigned.
We were absorbed in the collective shock of having lost her,
and the stain of having lost her to suicide. Dressed in black, we
gathered around her casket like the chorus in a Greek tragedy,
and the rabbi spoke for us. Inside of us there were words, long
sentences, curious narratives we had written out for ourselves
to hold ourselves together. But we were silent. If only animals
could talk, we sometimes think. What about humans in the face
of incoherent tragedy? What would we say?

I sat in the stiff white wooden folding chair at the foot of the gravesite, wearing sunglasses to conceal puffy eyes, bloated and uncomfortable. I was almost four months pregnant. I looked around and saw everyone from Kim's life: relatives, boyfriends, friends, and teachers. It was as if I were watching a movie where all the characters are recognizable but foreign. It seemed impossible that the girl with her stop-you-dead-in-your-tracks smile would no longer have a chance for happiness.

At the age of thirty-one my life was coming together. I was newly married and soon to have my own child. My husband, David, was launching his career as an attorney. I was a poet and a young editor at a New York publishing company. David's and my future stretched before us. My childhood had been shaped by the early loss of my father when I was two and the shadow of my mother's ensuing grief and melancholy; David's by the separation of a family after divorce. Our marriage offered each of us new promise. But in the years during which my life was finding its direction, Kim's life was coming undone.

During the week we sat shivah I found myself moving away from the exhaustion and emotions of the company gathered in the living room to go into Kim's bedroom, lie on the white bedspread stitched with red and blue and yellow flowers, and stare at the cathedral ceiling. It was as if her pain and despair flowed into my body and I was a young girl again, suffering from the anguish of wanting to be filled by another person.

When I was in grade school, years before Kim was born, there was a girl at our school with a head of beautiful curls and a lively, irresistible personality. She was popular, a straight-A student, and in sixth grade she was voted president of our school. The year she was president, we learned that she had killed herself. I couldn't help but wonder what would make a young girl want to take her life. Was there something happening in her family we hadn't known about? It was my first experience learning of a suicide, and the hushed news swept through our small community, imbuing us with sorrow, fear, and the awkward silence of bewilderment. Her brother went to law school with David and they were friends. When he and his family learned Kim had killed herself—even committing those two words to paper, "killed herself," makes me flinch—he came to our house to pay his respects. In his eyes I saw the broken world I had entered. I felt ashamed that all the years that I had known him, I had not really known him until that moment in the living room of my childhood home, when I knew his suffering. He acknowledged the pain of losing a sibling to suicide and, even as he comforted me, I remember that part of me thought, no, I can't, I won't be like you, because I would not accept that Kim was gone.

After the funeral and a week of shivah had passed, I returned to New York. I now lived in two realms: the realm of the ordinary world of getting up in the morning and making coffee, answering the phone, and going to work, the world of traffic and noise and obligations; and the realm of stopped time where my sister was dead and I was shrouded in the confusion of her loss.

Morning sickness continued. I managed to get down only saltine crackers and plain black tea, then vomited dry heaves, tasting the acids in my body. My baby gripped fiercely to my insides—sometimes I could barely catch my breath—but in spite of being sick, I was grateful to have a purpose outside the dark curtain that had dropped. I wondered if a baby inside me could die from the fear and pain the world held out. My obstetrician assured us that the womb was protection, like insulation in a house, but I did not believe him because I knew then it was possible to die from grief.

At night I could barely sleep—the minute I tried to shut my eyes I thought of what Kim had done. I couldn't stop picturing her alone in my mother's car, no one there to find her. To get through the night, I sometimes imagined the sky filled with a canopy of stars. I imagined that each star contained the soul of a girl or boy who had died too young, and the light the stars gave off was their brightness.

I slowly watched the slyness of daylight creep into the curtains before I exhausted myself to sleep and wondered why I should be living when my sister was gone. Surely she was. We'd laid her to rest in a beautiful cherry coffin.

My mother came to the city to visit David and me a few weeks later. We had planned the visit while I was still in Cleveland, hoping it would give her something to look forward to. We went to the Frick museum. We toured the painting gallery and stopped at Renoir's *Mother and Children,* the girls dressed in their muffs and fur hats. I looked at my mother and she looked back with that look we'd become accustomed to that acknowledged what we had lost. I did not know how we were going to survive Kim's death, but I also knew that grief was private and a journey each of us would have to make alone. I looked back at the painting of the mother with her arms outstretched as if to hold her daughters and protectively touched the little mound in my abdomen and then reached for my mother's hand. David and I wanted to have a family, but when I got pregnant we had only been married a year. The pregnancy had not been planned. We lived in a tiny one-bedroom apartment. We were worried about money and whether we were ready to begin a family, but still I was never afraid of motherhood. I had been in preparation my entire life.

I went to the bathroom at the museum, still filled by the bittersweet beauty of the paintings, and discovered I was bleeding. Spotting was common in pregnancy. We took a cab back to the apartment so I could lie down but soon I began to feel cramps in my abdomen, the same kind I felt every month when my body was working to expel the unfertilized egg, and the bleeding continued. I called my obstetrician and we took a cab to his office. My cervix had begun to dilate. My mother had taken DES when she was pregnant with me, a drug given to women to prevent miscarriages. The drug caused abnormalities in the reproductive systems of many daughters who were born from DES mothers. It wasn't until I was well into the pregnancy that we learned that I had a T-shaped uterus and an incompetent cervix resulting from DES exposure in utero. Before I was pregnant, my cervix and uterus had appeared normal.

Now I was admitted to the hospital for a procedure to stitch my cervix closed to prevent premature labor. For the remaining weeks of the pregnancy I was confined to bedrest at home. I was anxious that I might lose the baby who, as each day unfolded, had come to represent the possibility of a future swept clean of loss and pain. I tried not to think of Kim and her suicide. I told myself I would have years ahead to absorb it, but even though I tried to put it out of mind, I constantly thought of her. I worked in the mornings at home, reading manuscripts or editing. But within a short time I found myself staring at the cream walls of the living room, unable to focus.

I found I was looking forward to when the woman who cleaned our apartment came. Judy filled it with the smells of lemon oil and detergent, the bustle of lived life. One morning, while I lay on the living room couch on my side to enhance blood flow to the placenta, Judy came out of the bedroom where she'd been cleaning, holding an alarm clock. She said it was bad luck to have two clocks in one room and handed it to me. "It means a baby will die," she said. I quickly shrugged off the remark as silly superstition, but I never took the alarm clock back to the bedroom.

Occasionally, one of my friends stopped over to keep me company, bringing coffee and muffins, and gradually, though I didn't always want to, I found myself talking a little about Kim and what happened, but I discovered that talking about it often made me feel worse. Friends, meaning to help and offer sympathy, said stupid things. One of the most common was that suicide was her choice. How would it have been her choice, when she was only twenty-one years old? She hadn't yet developed the maturity to understand how to cope with her challenges and believe she could get through them or have the foresight to understand the repercussions of what she did. Another common response was that she was no longer suffering. But that she was no longer suffering was not comforting either. She was dead with no possibility of transforming, or transcending her anguish.

Though my friends wanted to help, I quickly learned I was navigating terrain few people understood. Each time I spoke of Kim I was reminded of the suffering she must have endured to have arrived at the place where she wanted to die and of the reality that I hadn't been paying close enough attention. When I saw the puzzled reactions of my friends, I thought they must have wondered the same thing. They seemed to want a clear reason to explain Kim's death. I didn't know what to say. For those whose lives are secure and steady, it must be difficult to imagine the inner fragility of an individual who chooses to die rather than live with despair. I imagine that the thought of suicide was something Kim had held up to the light like a many-sided crystal, thought about, toyed with in moments for years. How would my friends understand why Kim had taken her life and why I hadn't been able to help her? I didn't understand it myself. We do not want to comprehend that people may and do die of emotional pain, or to recognize the terror in ourselves when we cannot seem to help someone in despair—when our words are empty.

Instead of talking about my sister, I read books, hoping they'd shed light on what she had done and why. One was Jean-Jacques Rousseau's epistolary novel, *Julie, or the New Heloise.* Rousseau called suicide "a larceny committed against mankind." I agreed. I believed Kim had been stolen from us as our punishment for not having been aware of how deeply she was suffering. But I did not feel her act was a form of revenge against those of us who loved her. Rousseau's novel follows the fate of a tutor-turned-lover who years later reenters his pupil's life. Julie writes to her tutor that her "soul is oppressed with the weight of life. For a long time it has been a burden to me: I have lost everything that could have endeared it to me, only the sorrows remain to me." In her passionate letter Julie continues to lay out her decision to end her life and asks her tutor to give her reasons for living. "Speak to my heart; I am ready to hear you: but remember that despair cannot easily be fooled."

In his plea Julie's tutor outlines mankind's obligation to preserve life:

> You tire of living, and you say: life is an evil. Sooner or later you will be consoled, and you will say: life is good. You will be closer to the truth without reasoning any better: for nothing will have changed but you. That being so change right away, and since all the evil is in the ill disposition of your soul, amend your disorderly affections, and do not burn your house down to avoid the bother of putting it in order.

Julie's tutor tells her about the changeability of mood and outlook when in despair, how some days the world seems filled with possibility and other days everything is bleak, and he articulates a fundamental question when in a time of crisis: do we have it within us to put our house in order? The more important insight is the revelation that the evil vexing the individual lies within. To amend one's disorderly affections is to grasp those inner torments and gradually learn to understand their roots. Yet, when a person is caught in the vortex of anguish, helplessness, and self-doubt, achieving clarity in the moment is rarely possible. This conundrum is perhaps one of the most vexing psychological problems. Had Kim realized that she wasn't alone, had she been able to articulate her despair, she might possibly have survived the immediate crisis of pain that led her to take her life. But, unlike Rousseau's Julie, she had neither a tutor to offer her immediate instruction nor the gift of hindsight to know she might have come through.

Though Rousseau's words were thought-provoking and the novel tender, I closed the book filled with a fury I could barely name.

Throughout those days when I was confined to our apartment on bed rest, rubbing my growing abdomen to soothe my baby, trying to forget Judy's superstitious curse, I read pregnancy books to understand what had happened to mine and prayed my baby would survive. When I wasn't thinking about the baby, my mind skated back to thinking of Kim alone in the car on the night she died. It was one thing to know that she had been desperately unhappy, but the fact that she had wanted to die, that she had felt she had no future before her, was crushing. She was not a dramatic, self-involved person, acting out to get attention. She was kind and sweet, generally thinking of others before herself. How had she lost the will to live? I kept replaying over in my mind our last conversation, trying to find meaning from it.

LAST PHONE CALL

Just three days before Kim took her life I had talked with her from my office cubicle: a small desk, a cradle of books, a black telephone and its long cord I twisted in my hand, the same phone receiver I lifted to my ear when my mother called to tell me Kim was dead. It was Kim's and my last conversation and it

seemed significant. It was the 13th of April—T. S. Eliot's "cruellest month, breeding / Lilacs out of the dead land." It was my
birthday. Eliot, who suffered a mental breakdown, seemed to
know something about temperament and weather. Contrary to
what we may presume—that more suicides occur in the winter months—April, it turns out, is the cruelest. Suicide rates in
April are statistically 12 percent above the average for the rest
of the year.

"Hi Jilly," she said on the phone that morning. "How are
you?" Her voice was soft and sweet and just a little sad. "How's
Dave?"

I pictured her in her bedroom, propped up by pillows on
her bed, wearing a Cleveland Browns T-shirt and leggings,
her hair tied back in a high ponytail like any ordinary twenty-
one-year-old girl. For years afterward I played that phone
conversation over in my mind, wondering why I had not
known that she'd hit a wall and had been pulled under. Later
I learned that when a person has made a decision to end her
life, in the days before she may be privately saying goodbye.
I wondered whether on my birthday she already knew what
she was going to do three days later, if suicide was an option
she held out to console herself if her inner pain proved too
great to bear.

She asked me how I was feeling. I had just finished the first tri-
mester of my pregnancy and I was still sick from the moment
I woke up in the morning, retching into the toilet bowl, until
I went to bed at night. I kept crackers in my desk drawer, and
even as we spoke I tore the cellophane off one of the packets
while waiting for a wave of nausea to pass. Around me were

the sounds of typewriters and copy machines, phones ringing, and young assistants, just a year or two older than Kim, talking by the water cooler. I was aware that on the other side of the phone line, in the house I had grown up in, it was very quiet. Sometimes so quiet you could hear the floors creak.

Kim told me she was looking forward to being an aunt, and we planned that she would come visit when the baby was born. I fantasized about the special relationship she'd have with my child. I believed she'd babysit for my child, the way I had taken care of her when she was a baby and I was an adolescent, the circle continuing. "How are you?" I asked, hearing a slight turn in her voice.

"I'm OK," she said, in a voice that sounded far away, detached, as if she were underwater, swimming through a tangle of thick seaweed. You'll have your chance, I wished I'd said. I thought maybe my baby-in-waiting would give her hope. I knew that she wasn't doing well, but I had never considered she was suicidal. She had broken up with her boyfriend, whom she had come to depend on, and was in an acute mourning state where I imagined she felt like her skin was peeled off and she was more sensitive to the weather around her. I imagined that her day had begun with an unbearable ache in her chest because her boyfriend had left her—*my chest hurts and I don't understand why* was a refrain she'd written in her journal—an ache that in spite of getting up, eating breakfast, and talking to her older sister on the phone did not ease or go away.

I remember thinking that there was a time when I was her age and had my heart broken, during which I didn't know what my life was going to be, a time when I could not see or understand my own insecurities, and I thought to myself, soon it

won't hurt so much, you'll meet someone new, you'll turn the
corner and you won't remember how bad it felt. It will pass.
But instead, as we often do when we can't find the words, I
said very little, as if to give her the certain decorum she wanted
to maintain, not wanting to sound patronizing, relieved that
maybe what was between her and her boyfriend, Alan, was finally over.

"How's Mom?" I asked after a long pause.

"The same."

"I love you."

"I love you too."

Three days later she was gone.

A CRY FOR HELP

Did Kim want to die that April night, or was her act a cry for
help? This was one of the questions that haunted me. I thought
about the poet Sylvia Plath and the story of her suicide. In his
brilliant and moving memoir of Plath's suicide and his own
suicidal depression, *The Savage God,* Al Alvarez describes
the forces that shook Plath. "They had driven her to the thin
near edge of suicide," he writes of her first attempt. She was
nineteen. Those forces never fully let up, even when she was in
periods of intense creative mastery. When she took her life it
was very early one morning at the end of a long, bleak, isolat-
ing winter during which she'd been alone with her two small
children after her husband, the poet Ted Hughes, had left her
for another woman. The children were still asleep in their beds.
Before putting her head in the oven and drinking in its potent

fumes, she left food and a bottle of milk on the table, antici-
pating the nanny's arrival at nine a.m., knowing her children
would be taken care of. I thought of sentences in a journal I'd
read of hers where she described the agony and persistence of
despair like an owl's talons "clenching and constricting" her
heart. Alvarez was a friend of Plath's and an advocate for her
work; he'd published poems of hers in *The Observer.* He believed she saw thwarting death as a "physical challenge" and
said she had spoken about her past suicide attempts freely with
neither "hysteria nor an appeal for sympathy." Was it just luck
that her previous attempts had been unsuccessful? Alvarez sur-
mises that her fatal attempt may have been a cry for help. The
morning she died she left a note in the kitchen for the nanny
asking her to call the psychotherapist she had been attempting to contact, along with his phone number. The morning she
took her life, the mental pain was all-consuming, despite her
desire to protect and care for her children.

MIND OF WINTER

In trying to understand why some people have the ability to
endure intense despair while others succumb, I think of lines
from Wallace Stevens's "The Snow Man," where he writes,

> One must have a mind of winter,
> And have been cold a long time
> To behold the junipers shagged with ice,
> The spruces rough in the distant glitter

Of the January sun; and not to think
Of any misery in the sound of the wind,
In the sound of a few leaves,
Which is the sound of the land. . . .

In these lines Stevens describes the mind as a concentrated tool trained to withstand the blizzards of loneliness, trained to endure coldness and bleakness, in order to behold beauty without being overcome with misery. But in these lines I also infer an implicit layer of understanding, that each psyche adheres itself to the world in a different way, and that when what secures us is eroded the mind can cease to connect. These lines also made me wonder how much of resilience is genetically predetermined, or how much is socially or environmentally influenced, and how these factors interact with each other in an individual psyche.

PHANTOMS

In the evenings when I was on bed rest I tried not to talk too much about Kim with David. I could see it upset him. And it was good not to be always thinking about it. Instead we focused on our baby. We looked through baby catalogs and picked out cribs we liked; we talked about eventually moving into a bigger apartment. Sometimes I would look out our window at the garden with flowers blooming in the courtyard and I hoped that, through bringing new life into the world, my grief would lift. I searched for philosophical answers—there must be something to gain from Kim's death—but found none.

Nothing obliterated the uncomfortable feeling that I might have been able to change the outcome had I been aware of how deeply Kim was suffering. I looked at the petunias and pansies and the white and pink peonies regenerated from the decomposition of life in the soil. Subliminally I came to believe that Kim's essence was wrapped up in the baby growing inside me, the same way that the decomposition of one flower became the soil for another.

I talked to my baby on and off throughout the day and dreamed what she would look like. Our relationship had begun the minute I knew I was pregnant. I needed to prove to myself that raising a child in a sturdy household would help make up for what we had lost.

For the next month I was confined to our apartment while my child grew. I counted as each day passed by X-ing them off on my calendar. When I was thirty-one weeks along I awoke one morning, got up to go to the bathroom, and felt a rush of clear fluid down my leg. It was too soon. David called the doctor, who told us that I was in labor and we needed to get to the hospital. In the backseat of the cab David held my hand. My nervous excitement ceased the moment we saw the anxious look on the faces of the nurses and doctors in the emergency room. I was monitored for contractions and put on medications to stop the labor. The baby's lungs had not yet fully developed and the doctors wanted to give her as much time in the womb as possible. The next ten days were a blur of repeated stress tests where I heard the reassuring sounds of the baby's heartbeat, quick and steady, blood drawn so often that the veins in both my arms gave out and blood was drawn from a vein in my ankle, and sonograms. I watched mindless daytime television from the TV next to my hospital bed and looked through baby catalogs, waiting for the evening when David came by after work with his comforting air of reassurance. But I could see in the lines around his eyes that even he was worried.

When time ran out and the labor could no longer be controlled, I was rushed into the operating room for an emergency C-section. On the operating table I crouched over so that the nurse could put the epidural needle into my spine and thought that soon the long wait would be over. I was awake when they cut open my abdomen, when my baby was pulled through the slit, and when I heard her cry. Within minutes panic ensued. The placenta had adhered too tightly to my uterine lining. I lost blood when they tried to remove it, and to save my life I was given blood transfusions. A mask went over my face and I went under the ether of forgetfulness. When I awoke the world was never the same again.

The initial loss of amniotic fluid put weight on our baby's lungs. Ten minutes after she was born, her lungs collapsed and she died. I did not have a chance to hold the baby I had carried inside me for two hundred and seventeen days as she grew fingernails and little tufts of hair on her head, until after she was gone. When the nurse brought her into my hospital bed, she was wrapped in a striped pink flannel blanket and the cotton pink cap I now keep pressed in a folder in my drawer along with the Polaroid snapshot the nurse took of her. When she was placed in my arms I could feel that she was still warm with the last breaths of life. I looked at her and marveled that she had my wide forehead, little almond-shaped eyes, snow-white skin. "She's beautiful," David said. I read later that primates who have lost their baby carry the body around with them for days, nuzzling and cradling the corpse as if it were still alive, unable to let go, aware perhaps of death's brutal supremacy. When the nurse took her from my arms, every neuron in my body responded as if we were still attached invisibly. The trauma of losing my firstborn and the loss of Kim to suicide have forever become tangled like threads in a rope. There are things in life we are powerless to control or change—"the ungraspable phantoms of life." For two days I lay in the hospital room staring at the fluorescent lights on the ceiling, unable to be consoled.

FUNERAL CLOTHES

The night before Kim's funeral my younger sister Cindy and I braced ourselves and drove to the funeral home to see Kim laid out in her casket. My mother and my older sister, Laura, chose not to come, wanting to preserve in their memory their own images of Kim when she was alive. Under Jewish law caskets are closed. It is considered disrespectful to stare at someone who cannot look back at you. Therefore in the Jewish tradition there is no visitation. However, if close family members feel the need to see the deceased one last time prior to the funeral, they may do so privately. I felt compelled to go, not wanting Kim to be alone. That morning my sisters and I had painstakingly picked out a white satin jacket, white pants, and her new pair of white boots—for some reason we decided to bury her in white as if she were a young bride and we were preparing for her wedding in the underworld. My mother could not partake in the funeral arrangements. She could barely function.

Though I had many fears, I had no fear of seeing Kim in her coffin. It was strange to see her face fixed in time, like a statue, all the beauty of life taken from her. Ever since then I haven't been able to pass by a human sculpture without thinking of the sculptor's desire to re-create the beloved as though to imbue her again with life.

Three and a half months later, on August 1, I held my baby daughter wrapped in her funeral blanket and pink cap—hospital flannel—in my arms, making sure in those few moments to fill her with a lifetime of love. Before the baby died, we thought of naming her after Kim, but I worried about the legacy of naming a child after a suicide. Instead we called her Isabel. Some religions believe that it takes a certain period of time for the soul to escape the body. If you've ever seen a person embalmed in a casket, you have no doubt the soul has fled.

WHAT MIGHT HAVE BEEN
AND WHAT HAS BEEN

After Isabel died I was overwhelmed by physical, visceral grief. It was as if I still wanted to believe that the baby was alive and would be returning home, in the same way that I wanted to believe that Kim was still physically alive and that my life could begin again. When I walked into our apartment after leaving the hospital, I could not accept that my baby was gone, too. I spoke to Isabel in my mind, staring at the picture the nurse had taken of her and feeling tremors in my uterus as if she were still snug and safe inside me. At night when I was trying to sleep I sometimes thought I heard her cry, and I got up and walked around the apartment in a daze. Once when I was taking the crosstown bus, my body still carrying my pregnancy weight, a woman cradling a baby took the seat next to mine and asked me when I was due. I found myself unable to tell her that my baby had died, and we spoke together like young mothers about mundane matters of baby care, about brands of strollers and snugglies, about whether we wanted to return to work or be stay-at-home moms. In other more lucid moments, I was completely aware of what I had lost. I played the days and weeks of my pregnancy and the last ten days in the hospital over and over again, trying to figure out what went wrong, as if I could reverse the past. At night I wrapped myself around David's body on the narrow couch and pretended to watch the movies we'd rented, but I thought only of those people I had loved, however briefly, who were no longer within my reach. I broke down into tears sometimes in the bathroom stall in restaurants or on the subway. On other days I woke up and felt better and thought, I'm past this now, and then another wave of grief would seize hold. When I look back at that time it strikes me that I was temporarily crazy.

GIVER OF LIGHT

The minute my doctor gave us the OK to try to have another baby, we began in earnest. I did not know what else to do with the dreams and desires that had grown along with Isabel inside me. David, too, was out of sorts. I sometimes saw the sad look in his eyes when we passed a baby in a carriage on the streets. A year of mourning passed and I became pregnant again. Then, on New Year's Eve, we were having friends over for supper. While I was dressing I looked at myself in the mirror. My abdomen, where my baby had been hibernating for six months, seemed smaller to me. Later I noticed that the thumping inside me had slowed. The next day I called the obstetrician and went in for a stress test. The baby was in jeopardy. My uterine lining was thin, another anomaly from being exposed to DES, and the baby wasn't getting adequate nourishment through the placenta. Within hours I was admitted to the hospital and prepped for an emergency C-section. Our son Samuel was born so tiny he looked like a frog. He weighed under two pounds. When I saw him in the ICU, every inch of his body was taped up to machines. Yet, when I looked at his little face it was clear he had David's nose. In spite of the fact that he was so tiny, I was enraptured. I had read that babies could survive at twenty-six weeks. But six hours later I was awakened by one of the doctors in the ICU to the news that the baby's kidneys had shut down and he had died. How was it possible? I could barely look at David, knowing my body had failed to sustain our son. Life was fragile and my own baby had not been safe inside me.

I couldn't bear to speak to anyone. I spent the better part of the evenings staring out into the blackness beyond the windows. During those initial months, the loss of the babies seemed to eclipse the loss of Kim. Now, too, there was little hope that I could carry another child. I learned that I was at risk if we underwent another pregnancy. My obstetrician feared that my uterus would rupture and, in order to save my life, I'd have to have an emergency hysterectomy. I grew fixated on the fear that I might never have the chance to be a mother and have a child. I was terrified of what else might happen. When David went to work I feared something bad would happen to him. I was afraid to leave my apartment, only traveling the circumference of my block to pick up groceries or drop off David's shirts at the dry cleaner. The *DSM-IV (Diagnostic Statistical Manual of Psychological Disorders)* calls this condition post–traumatic stress syndrome. But I prefer to call it simply disbelief. There are certain things in life for which we can never be prepared.

During the day when David was at work and I was still at home recovering from the C-section, my breasts still full and leaking milk, I turned down the blinds and curled up on the couch. My abdomen was sore from the surgery. On my panty line was a long crescent-shaped gash held together by silver staples that glinted in the creases of my skin. This was where I had been opened, the little envelope of flesh my child had been pulled through. The skin around the wound was puffy and purple. How fragile the body is, I thought. How fragile we all are. With each loss, it seemed as though I mourned the loss of Kim all over again. I was aware of the responsibility of bringing a child into the world and the fragility of life and the bewilderment of consciousness. Each day I thought I would not be able to get up and do the simple tasks that awaited me; nevertheless, each day I somehow managed to remove myself from the couch and embrace some form of living, whether it was simply doing a load of laundry or turning on my computer, and each day little by little I began to feel better. But grief wound tightly inside my muscles. Once on holiday at a resort in the Caribbean where we had gone to recuperate weeks after we had lost Samuel, the shadow life of our babies with us, David surprised me with the gift of a massage. When the massage therapist

began to massage my shoulders, I was overcome by uncontrollable sobs, as if my body had been armor for my grief and the
massage had loosened the floodgates.

Perhaps it was the insistent sound of the waves crashing at night outside the window at the resort, and, later, once
we'd returned home, the way light teased through the trees on
the block, the sound of laughter coming from a playground in
Central Park, and the need for company again, that allowed me
gradually to venture a few more blocks in the neighborhood, to
put one foot in front of the other and permit myself to live in
a world bereft of my babies and my sister. I don't know how
David was able to make me laugh again. I don't know how we
had the courage to embrace hope. But, eventually, fearful of another high-risk pregnancy and another loss, we decided to adopt
a child, and it was as if God decided we'd had enough, and we
were blessed with a beautiful baby boy. Lucas. Giver of light.

The weeks before our son Lucas was to be born we were frightened that his birth mother would decide to keep him, and we
couldn't have blamed her had that been her choice. Though for
months I had window-shopped along Madison Avenue looking longingly in the too-expensive baby-shop windows and
dreaming of blue and yellow outfits, flannel blankets, and little
onesies, we decided not to buy a single diaper, plastic bottle,
or rattle. It was impossible for us to believe that happiness was
waiting for us just around the corner, that very soon we'd be
parents. But Lucas's birth mother had made her decision with
care and thought. We had spent time with her before she gave
birth and she had come to trust David and me. In spite of the
love she had for her baby, she knew she could not raise him. She

did not change her mind. The day we brought Lucas home was the happiest day of our lives. That night our friends brought over a bassinet and some baby clothes. David went to Duane Reade and stocked up on diapers and baby bottles. The first few nights I was afraid to close my eyes and sleep out of fear that Lucas would not be there when I awoke. Sometimes startled in my sleep, I woke up in the middle of the night and put my hand close to his mouth to make sure I could feel the warmth of his breathing.

On the day of Lucas's bris I had not yet left the house, even to go around the corner for groceries. It was two or three days since we had brought Lucas home. I decided that morning to get my hair cut at a beauty salon two blocks away. As the stylist blew out my hair I felt myself growing anxious, near panic, at being apart from Lucas. I didn't have the patience to let her finish. I walked quickly to our apartment and into the living room and saw that he was sound asleep in his bassinet where I had left him. David, who knew me well, at first looked at me perplexed, then lovingly rolled his eyes and shook his head. "He's fine," he said. When Lucas awoke, I picked him up and remembered a picture of Kim when she was a baby that was propped on the counter in my mother's living room. I was startled by how much they looked alike, how similar the solid feel of their bodies in my arms and their damp baby smell. Maybe it was the blue eyes, the light coloring, and the perfectly round baby's head they shared. I thought that Kim's soul had been reincarnated inside our baby, and a wave of peace I had not experienced in years washed over me. When my older sister, Laura, saw Lucas for the first time, she felt the same thing. "Kimmy brought him to you," my mother said.

Now that Lucas was in our lives I thought we could begin anew. We made sure his little room was perfect. We installed carpet over the wood floor, painted the room, picked out a crib and a black and white mobile for him to train his eyes. David's sister brought us a white rocking chair. There was nothing I liked more than to wake up to Lucas in his crib cooing to the play of light. That first summer with him was like a dream. We were so very happy. My mother likes to tell this story. When Lucas was a baby and David and I were together, he didn't know which of our arms he'd rather be in. I'd hold him and then he'd see David and he'd reach out his arms for David to hold him, and then once in David's arms he'd look back at me and reach his arms out wanting me to hold him. He seemed not to be content until he'd acted out this little ritual. Was he afraid that one of us would feel hurt if he wanted the other? I think it was more primal. He wanted us both. One would not do without the other. We had formed a triangle and he was at the center. We were the two figures who defined him.

BABYHOOD

In spite of my happiness I woke up some mornings feeling dread. Something was missing. I lived with the strange fear that there was worse to come, that I did not deserve the happiness that Lucas had brought to our lives. Sometimes when I sat in the rocker with Lucas in my arms and fed him a bottle, his little fingers picking at the skin around my cuticles—a soothing habit he had discovered—I inadvertently called him Kim. At night I had dreams about her and in my dream she was a little girl and she was calling out to me.

When I awoke I remembered how she used to crawl into my girlhood twin bed in the early morning when she was two or three wearing her yellow nightgown, which stuck to her body with static. I remembered the feel of her cold little toes touching my skin and the sound of her soft voice as she said my name. I recalled the intensity of her crystal-blue eyes, the softness of her baby-fine blond hair, and the pure pleasure of her squeals of delight. It was so easy to protect her then.

I couldn't accept that she was no longer in our world, just as it was difficult to accept that the two babies we had conceived and I had carried inside me for months were no longer alive. I suppose no one is truly dead when we go on loving them. Théophile Gautier, the French Romantic poet, art critic, and story writer, knew something about the tragedy of suicide. He was also a journalist and wrote the obituary for his friend, the poet Gérard de Nerval, whose suicide shook him and inspired him to write a story called "The Poet." Later, in another story collected in a volume called *My Fantoms*, he made one of the remarkable declarations of his fiction:

> Nothing, in fact, actually dies: everything goes on existing, always. No power on earth can obliterate that which has once had being. Every act, every word, every form, every thought, falls into the universal ocean of things, and produces a ripple on its surface that goes on enlarging beyond the furthest bounds of eternity.

I felt driven to understand what had happened to Kim. She was a phantom always near me; I sometimes felt as if she was beckoning me to try and piece together her story. Not only was I frightened for Kim, because she existed for me as if she were alive, still in psychic pain, but I feared for Lucas as well. If I didn't understand why Kim had taken her life, how would I understand the inner world of my own child? What might go wrong if I was not paying close enough attention? Each of us has veins of vulnerability inside us from experiences that have shaped us, producing our own unconscious nighttime dramas. Who knew what experiences would stay with him and where his vulnerabilities and fault lines would lie?

Kim's suicide has made me a vigilant mother, perhaps at times too overly conscious of the effects of the actions of my life and my husband's, the state of our marriage, on our child's internal development. Perhaps this is the legacy of losing a loved one to suicide. I know that the worst can happen. The suicide's strangest gift is what she leaves to the living. I know that my actions have consequences, though we can never be certain how our actions will manifest in our children. The tragedy is that the price of learning this knowledge is so high. Vows ought to be written before a child is born—I will always take care of you. I will put you before myself at all costs. I will never leave you. Like so many mothers everywhere, I hoped that by making these promises and knowing them to be true, they would carry us through. At night I would hold Lucas in my arms in the white rocker in his room as he fell asleep.

During this time, to understand what happened to Kim, I was still reading all I could find about suicide in fiction, poetry, and psychoanalytical texts. But too often in the psychoanalytic literature, the pain of the mental anguish and its consequences seemed abstract and intellectualized. Where was the young child who was no different from any one of us and whose life seemed filled with possibility and hope? What happened to her? There had to be more to the story.

I knew intuitively that the roots of Kim's unhappiness began in her childhood—even further, back to my own childhood and perhaps to my mother's before us, and to Kim's father's and what little we knew of his history. I needed to thread those histories together to comprehend where and when the security of her inner world began to unravel. I sensed it was those places of emotional vulnerability she crashed against throughout the difficult teenage years. I replayed the story of Kim's last few days, still thinking that if I could pinpoint what went wrong I could change the past. But I knew that what had happened went deeper.

part two

HOUSE OF WATER

My mother was a child bride, married when she was nineteen, a mother by the time she was twenty-one, a widow at twenty-four. She was raised to be a devoted wife and mother. Her own mother died when she was nine years old and she was raised frugally by her father, a bank teller; her grandmother; and later her aunts, Harriet and Florence. She was an adored and fussed-over child. She recorded her dates and sorority dances in high school in scrapbooks, bringing home a matchbook or a corsage to paste into her book. When she met my father, and then married him, it seemed like her life was just beginning.

We lived in Shaker Heights, Ohio, an upper-middle-class suburb. It was the late fifties and early sixties. My father was in real estate. His family, Russian Jews who had fled a city in Lithuania called Vilna, landed on Ellis Island. They first lived in Hoboken, New Jersey, and eventually moved to Cleveland. My mother's family was of Hungarian descent. My parents were first- and second-generation Americans, respectively, the Jewish nouveau riche, whose parents had lived through world wars. They aspired to make a good living in a new land, away from loss and suffering, and raise good Jewish-American children. My mother was in a bowling league, played mahjong, waited for my father to come home from work, got her hair done every Friday at the beauty parlor, and went for manicures. She adored my father. She used to boast that of all the women he could have had he had chosen her. She said that my father used to come home from the real estate company where he worked to have lunch with her so they could be together. She told us how much he loved his daughters. Photographs do not lie; there is an ease of expression in their faces, a shared look of mutual comfort.

When she met my father she felt as if it was *bershert,* a Yiddish word meaning that God had intervened. I don't believe my mother ever recovered from the loss of her first love. Years later she would say to me that still she was lucky, that most people never experience the kind of love she and my father shared. She still wears her diamond engagement ring. It is hard to comprehend that she was only twenty-four when her husband died of a sudden heart attack and all of it crumbled. I don't know how my mother managed with three young girls under the age of four. I can only suppose what those early months after my father died were like. I imagine my mother stayed in bed, paralyzed by her grief. I know that she went to see a psychiatrist and was given Valium, a drug she came to depend on. My relatives offered support when they could, though they had their own families to attend to. Every Sunday we went for brunch at Aunt Harriet's and Uncle Joe's, and over a table set with elegant china and silver, eating noodle kugel and brisket, Uncle Joe told us funny stories that made us laugh and Aunt Harriet scolded him playfully. The unasked question hovered in the room: how would we survive? Without a college diploma or any working experience, my mother eventually did what most women of her generation, raised to be wives and mothers, would have done and what her family encouraged her to do. She went on a quest to find a new man to replace my father. She wasn't yet thirty. She was a beautiful woman with wavy dark hair she wore in a flip and with a model's figure, and she exuded a warm, caring glow. I suppose some men must have felt sorry for her and sensed her vulnerability, which might have made her more attractive. Preparing for her dates seemed, at least then, to make her happy and hopeful.

My mother tried to do a good job of it after my father died, but it was tough. In our community it seemed as if she was the only single mom around—it was the early sixties. Our childhood was filled with longing and loss and, underlying that, a pervasive, nagging desperation. From the outside we looked like the rest of the kids on our block. We went to school, played kick-the-can in the backyard, went to ballet lessons and to temple on Saturdays. But inside our house things were terribly wrong. My mother was heartsick and grief stricken and her sickness made her listless. In addition to her heartache, I think she must have been angry that my father had died and that she had been deprived of the more privileged life that friends of hers and my father's were leading. I'm certain my father's death reopened the grief my mother had suffered when she lost her own mother. At that time there was no language in which to explain or understand extended periods of languid melancholy. If her melancholy manifested in what we would now characterize as depression, I'm not sure she even knew. In that era, depression was shameful and something to keep hidden in the privacy of one's home. If you were mentally ill you were often hospitalized or, worse, put in an institution.

My mother often retreated to her bed, either suffering from a migraine, or quieted by a pill she'd taken for her nerves, or recovering from an evening out with a date when she may have had too much to drink. I'm sure, at least in those hours, it was the only way she knew to escape from her intense grief and frustration over a life she hadn't predicted or planned. Sometimes, when my mother was in bed sleeping throughout the day, we three girls played in the living room, stacking up the packets of Winston or Pall Mall cigarettes she kept on the living room table or making houses out of decks of cards, waiting for her to wake up and begin her day, though by then it might be dusk.

I was a quiet and inward girl. I did not like anyone to notice me. My mother says that I would walk down the stairs and look at the ceiling if we had company in the house. Cindy and I were "Irish twins," born only fourteen months apart. We shared a bedroom together and every morning walked to school side by side. I was afraid of birds, and when we walked to school and a flock of pigeons or a swoop of sparrows narrowed our path, Cindy scared the birds away before I walked past. She had knock-knees and was skinny, with a short pixie haircut. I was a little chubby with a round face and curly hair. While I was pensive and reserved, she was easily distracted, the kid at school who was disorganized, never able to stay still. Laura was a serious, contemplative child, with long brown hair and blue eyes and freckles on her pale skin. She liked to spend time in her bedroom playing with her paper dolls or reading. But when my mother went out we would go into her room at night and pile onto her bed until we fell asleep. We were pillars for each other, holding one up when another would fall.

————————

Money was a problem. I knew we lived off the social security checks we received from the government and with some help from relatives. For a time my mother was a receptionist in a doctor's office, but that job didn't last long. I don't remember feeling we had much of anything to sink our teeth into, anything to hold on to or call our own. I remember feeling that my destiny somehow depended on my mother and not being at all sure that my mother had the kind of strength I could rely on. There were times, too, when my mother had more hope and our future seemed more optimistic, but then she would fall, hopeless about her situation. She suffered unbearable migraines. During these periods, the house was messy and disorganized. Without the energy to go to the grocery store or cook, she sent us to Mawby's or Manners at the corner for hamburgers. The bills stacked up and she worried about how she was going to pay them. During my childhood it seemed that our house was floating adrift on a turbulent sea of uncertainty, and we were all waiting for someone to reel us in.

There were many men who came in and out of our lives in those years; it was hard to keep them straight. But when I was in the fifth grade, my mother came home one afternoon from the justice of the peace in city hall married to a man we had never met. In a whirlwind of excitement she showed us her opal wedding ring. Later she put on her makeup and fixed her hair in the little bathroom off her bedroom, getting ready for her new husband to come pick her up. When he walked in the door, tall and broad, sandy-colored hair, a space between his two front teeth when he smiled, piercing blue eyes, wearing a blue blazer and slacks, my stomach tightened. "You girls are just about as pretty as your mother," he said in a boisterous voice, a little too loud for our house. Within less than an hour they were off again. They went on a honeymoon to Acapulco and left my sisters and me with a babysitter who was a stranger. I was afraid my mother might never come back. When she did, our new surrogate father moved into our house with us as if things had never been any different. I'm not sure whether my mother knew much about him. The only things he brought with him were a black leather Eames chair for our living room and suitcases filled with his clothes. He was Irish Catholic and, based on the kind of car he drove and his cashmere sweaters and expensive suits, worked in what appeared to be a lucrative business in the food sector that involved traveling and often took him away from home. Once he mentioned something about vending machines and cafeterias. Every time I came across a vending machine with Clark Bars, M&Ms, and Doublemint chewing gum behind glass, I thought of him. But the truth be told, I had no idea what his line of business was. His work life, like so much about him, was never part of the conversation. There was an aura of mystery about it that intrigued me. He was part of the larger, more powerful patrician world outside the domestic life of my family where I imagined men conducted important and complicated business transactions. His blue eyes twinkled when he smiled. He drank a lot, laughed hard, and had a temper. My mother came to life in his presence.

We were possessive of our mother and apprehensive about our stepfather. We weren't used to a lot of rules in the house, and our stepfather could be rigid and angry when we didn't immediately do what was expected of us. Once when we were called down for supper and one of us refused to come down, he climbed up the stairs, threw open the bedroom door, and literally dragged the dissenter into the hallway as she screamed for him to let go. He swore at her and then at my mother, who was trying to intercede. My mother was caught in the middle, sometimes defending her husband, sometimes one of her daughters, and there was tension because of it.

It wasn't that I minded having him around; he just made me nervous. I felt I had to tiptoe around him, contain myself so as not to do anything that might make him leave us. Yet there was always anxiety in the air that he might. I suspect he must have loved my mother to have agreed to be saddled with three young children to support, along with the two we learned he had from his first marriage.

I don't remember him talking much about his two other children. In fact, I don't remember him talking about anything except for the things he liked, good food and wine, fine restaurants, football, and golf. There seemed to be an unknown universe that existed for him outside our house, and it enchanted me with its veil of mystery. Who was this strange man? Our house was the place where he slept at night if he wasn't traveling, where he showered, came downstairs and playfully squeezed my mother or one of us girls or announced seemingly out of the blue that he was crazy about our mother. I was caught off guard by his cheerfulness, the strong and certain sound of his voice, and his extroverted personality. In the mornings he was usually gone before we left for school. He'd come home sometimes in the evenings for supper, but more often he'd pick my mother up and take her out to expensive restaurants with his friends, as if they were still dating.

The first year or two of their marriage my mother and stepfather were happy. Even as a child, I knew there was a strong attraction between them. They flirted and laughed together. Being in their presence filled me with a happy kind of loneliness. We didn't quite feel included in their union, but my mother no longer worried about how we were going to survive financially and she was calmer and more at peace. I too felt more secure. My mother dressed for her new husband and he bought her jewelry, designer clothes, and expensive perfume; she reciprocated by giving him attention. Now we sat around the dinner table and my mother made elaborate meals of roast beef or lamb, when before, if she were up to cooking at all, she made us simple meals of tuna noodle casserole, wiener goulash, or Kraft macaroni and cheese. My mother placed the roast from the oven on a butcher block and we watched the man who ruled the table carve it, the red bloody juices running along the knife. I stared at the rare beef on my plate and was reminded of the cows we used to see when we drove past farms in the rural areas outside of Cleveland. When my mother and stepfather weren't looking I took bites of the meat and spat them into my napkin. Looking at my stepfather, it amazed me how a home-cooked meal could make someone happy, and yet there was happiness, that elusive thing that had dodged my family most of our lives, incarnated in the boisterous and carnivorous man sitting at the head of our table.

Once he decided he was going to teach me how to ride a bike. For my birthday, he bought me a purple Schwinn with tassels on the handlebars. I was anxious that I wouldn't be able to learn and would disappoint him. But before I knew it he was by my side, holding the back of the bike seat and the steering wheel, running beside me to keep up as I peddled. I liked him hovering over me, protective and overbearing, making sure I wasn't going to fall. When he let go of the bike, my heart beat with the rat tat tat of accomplishment. When I rode back to him, he beamed. I didn't mind having him around. Having a man at home had its advantages.

There were other ways in which our life was to change, all kinds of dreams and plans. One was the possibility of buying a new house. Though the thought of leaving the white house with the black shutters and the red door that had come to define my only port of safety made me feel slightly afraid, there was also before us the idea of grandeur that might await if we moved. Once I remember going house shopping, my mother and newly appointed dad in the front seat and me and my two sisters squashed into the back, forming the trio of "girls" we had come to be defined as, as if we were indeed one person, my stepfather singing to the songs of Frank Sinatra on the car radio. But once we entered the prefabricated model home that smelled like sawdust and fresh paint in some suburb so new that there were only the thinnest of trees lining the street— unlike the abundant elms and sprawling oaks on our block— my heart sank. I missed my bed that overlooked our backyard and our rusted swing set and the view of my best friend Martha's roof. I was relieved when the plans to move petered out and instead they settled on expanding our kitchen.

What was it like to have a man in a house that had once belonged to all women? Bedroom doors were now mostly kept shut. The newly acquired liquor cabinet in our house was now filled with the finest scotches, a wine rack in our living room housed with expensive cabernets and ports. A new color television was installed in the living room, my mom decided to take cooking lessons, and we girls went about life the way we always had, walking the few blocks to school, coming home again, going back to school, bouncing a bright-colored ball back and forth on the sidewalk or playing hopscotch. Who knew what they talked about or shared? Those conversations were held in the privacy of their bedroom or when they went out on their date nights. Why of all the men who came in and out of our house had our mother chosen this foreign and glamorous one from among the tepid, innocuous fathers I was used to, the ones who belonged to my friends from school, who took the rapid transit downtown to work wearing gray suits and came home every night at six with their briefcases and settled down to read the newspaper and on Saturdays mowed their rectangular-shaped front lawns?

After the first year, they started going to Saturday night parties where cocktails like Rusty Nails, Pink Ladies, and crème de menthe were served. For my mother this meant a new social set. But something more must have occurred on those nights because when they came home they fought. We weren't used to the sound of a man cursing in our house. It frightened me how my stepfather could wake up cheerful and sunny and by the end of the evening turn mean and angry. Once they fought terribly. It may have started because my stepfather was late coming home and my mother was angry over something he said, but as the night wore on the argument grew louder and more intense and complicated. Sometimes in the afternoons on Sunday they fought while we girls secluded ourselves in the damp basement. We played farm or house. Once we crayoned an entire wall of the basement as a surprise for our mother and got into scads of trouble. We played Crazy Eights, Jacks, and Cat's Cradle. It was sweet and sometimes hollow, those hours waiting for the grown-ups to settle. Another time my stepfather broke down a door during one of their fights. Even though I knew that he was gone too much and I was afraid of his temper, I remember wishing that my mother wouldn't get mad. I worried that she would only arouse his temper further and push him away.

Over the months he had been living with us I had grown attached to him. In spite of the tension he caused, I didn't want my mother to be alone again and our household to fall apart. When I feared he was going to leave us I concocted a fantasy in my head, one that Freud would have been proud of—that my stepfather was going to take me away so that I could live with him. Even though I knew in my heart I could never leave my mother, I was afraid of what would happen to her, and to us, if we were on our own again. I prayed things between them would work out. There was nothing I liked more than the Sunday mornings when he singled me out to go to the donut shop, where I could pick out any kind of donut I wanted—his nature was to buy two dozen instead of one. His favorite was raspberry jelly. He popped them in his mouth as if they were candy. It was the first time any man had shown me attention and I'm embarrassed to say that I coveted even the gruff and sometimes dismissive nature of his temperament. He didn't like anyone or anything to get in the way of his plans or how he felt things should be done. In looking back, I see how the seeds of attachment to a father can form in a young girl.

One weekend a few months into the marriage he brought his two other children who lived in Pittsburgh to our house to visit. His daughter was a year older than Laura and his son was a year or two younger than Cindy. They both had the same space between their front teeth that their father had. She wore pink plastic-framed cat's-eye glasses that turned up on the sides. He was boyish and preppy. He had a buzz cut with a cowlick in the center of his forehead and a quirky smile. We were tentative around one another, barely speaking the first day, staying close to our respective parents. His daughter was slightly withdrawn and seemed to want attention and affection from her father, though he would mostly just tease her. The boy roughhoused with our new puppy—a husky we instantly fell in love with that had one blue eye and one green eye—that our stepfather had brought home one day from a farm as a surprise for us. I worried that they wouldn't like my mother. She was sexy and feminine, not the maternal portrait of motherhood I was sure they were used to. She was tentative around them, and slightly flirtatious, as if she didn't know what her role should be, and spent most of the time in the kitchen or in her bedroom. That weekend seemed to last forever. My mother and stepfather made us an elaborate dinner of coq au vin and thin and buttery almond cakes—they were in the kitchen for hours. The next day my stepfather loaded all of us into his car and took us shopping and bought us four girls identical red, black, and white checkered dresses to wear. He bought his son a preppy V-neck sweater in the same color combination. It was as if by dressing us alike he thought we'd become a family. That night we went out in our new outfits to a fancy restaurant for dinner. I was relieved when the weekend was over and his children were packed away in the Cadillac and driven back home to Pittsburgh, where they lived with their mother. Who was she? She became another ghostly presence that took possession of my mind. I wondered what she must have been like to have married my stepfather and then not been able to keep him. Another time we all went on a vacation together to a boardwalk seaside town in New Jersey where I got sick over too much saltwater taffy and tepid hotdogs, the jerk of the surf and hours packed like sardines in the back of the car that smelled nauseatingly of fresh leather while my mother and stepfather affectionately teased each other in the front seat. I was glad when we finally returned home.

After that trip his children no longer came to see us, as if the audition hadn't worked and it had been quietly understood that we were never destined to become a family.

No matter the affection I had come to feel for my stepfather, his marriage to my mother was on shaky ground. There were periods that seemed calm followed by weeks of turbulence when my mother might be found holding back tears at the sink doing dishes, until my stepfather, carrying a bouquet of roses, bounded in the door after having been away for days, and she would brighten. But if my mother said the wrong thing, suddenly he'd erupt again and walk out of the house, slamming the door behind him so hard I heard the glass rattle. Sometimes he didn't phone her for days and my mother would be beside herself with worry. I began to wonder what made him stay away.

The only truly good thing that eventually came out of that marriage was a beautiful, blond baby girl, our new sister Kim, an innocent brought into a family already damaged by loss and a marriage held together by a thread.

When my mother found out she was pregnant with Kim, she hoped the new baby would help to bring our family together. Now there'd be a baby one part hers and one part her husband's. Or perhaps she felt that her new husband was beginning to stray and hoped the baby would keep him focused on our family. One morning, soon after my mother discovered she was pregnant, our new puppy was asleep in our hallway. Laura reached down to kiss him and, startled, he took a bite out of her cheek. Before Kim was born, as if a harbinger of what was later to come, we gave the puppy away because my mother was frightened he might harm the baby.

Pregnancy suited my mother. She glowed in her newfound happiness. She went on a campaign to prepare for the new baby. My sister Laura's room became the baby's room. Cindy and I moved downstairs to the den-turned-new-bedroom and Laura took over the bedroom I had shared with Cindy. My mother wanted the nursery to mimic the outdoors. She had green shag carpet installed for grass, painted the walls blue for sky. Laura drew large daisies on the blue walls with a pencil and the rest of us painted the petals yellow and orange and white with long green stems. My mother ordered a miniature white picket fence that we hammered into the walls as a border around the room. She found an antique wooden cradle at a flea market and had a new mattress made to fit it. She insisted that newborns needed to sleep in a narrow space to imitate the enclosed world of the womb. She ordered a white changing table and a chest of drawers. It wasn't until Kim was a teenager, when we other kids had left home and Kim moved her bedroom downstairs, that the room was stripped of its white fence and shag carpet, and the colored daisies of her walls painted over.

The day Kim was born her father was nowhere to be found. I accompanied my mother and our babysitter, Olivia, to the hospital. When our stepfather moved in he had brought Olivia with him to look after our house a few times a week. She used to clean his apartment. Olivia was like our second mother. I loved her dark, soft skin and abundance of girth and heart. I would stay down in the basement with her for hours while she ironed our clothes and talked about her daughter and the two foster boys she took in, the goings-on at her church. We kids lived for her homemade pancakes the size of silver dollars. Once she took me on a trip to Disneyland with her church group.

Unlike Olivia, my mother rarely filled the house with the chatter of daily life. It wasn't her way. We were either in a state of crisis or, if things were going well, left to ourselves. Because things were physically and emotionally always falling apart, Olivia used to call our house "the house that Jack built" and laugh after she said it. She would call Kim "baldy" because she was born with peach fuzz on her scalp instead of hair. I sat in the waiting room with Olivia while my mother endured her labor. After my mother gave birth, my stepfather walked into the waiting room, having finally been located, with his conciliatory bouquet of flowers in his hand. I accompanied him to my mother's hospital room, where she lay with the baby in her arms, and when she saw him she tucked away her disappointment and brightened. "She looks just like you," my mother said. He looked down at the two of them and beamed.

My mother wanted to name the baby Elizabeth, and my stepfather wanted to name her Kim; so they settled on Kim Elizabeth. When they brought Kim home from the hospital, ensconced in our stepfather's arms, we sisters flew down the stairs to greet her. We couldn't take our eyes off of her. She was so beautiful and perfect. We all felt that, with the new baby, things at home might get better.

But Kim's father was away again nine months later on the day my mother had to take her to the hospital. I held her in the backseat as my mother drove. Kim's fever had spiked so high she was listless. In the hospital she was diagnosed with meningitis. For three days my mother remained by her bedside, praying she wouldn't die or suffer brain damage. She made a pact with God to save her daughter's life: If she were allowed to live, my mother would try harder to make her marriage work. Perhaps by then my mother had already lost her husband. It's possible that she had never had him. I, too, sat up all night in my bed and prayed for Kim's life.

THE SUNDANCE KID

When he wasn't teeing off for eighteen holes of golf at the country club or drinking swigs of scotch from a flask passed around in the stands at the Cleveland Browns games where he had season tickets, or away on one of his business trips, my stepfather gave Kim his attention, though I don't remember him ever taking her for a stroll in her carriage around the block or changing a diaper. Of course, men in those days rarely did. She had his light coloring and blue sparkling eyes and soft pudgy white skin rippling with healthy baby fat. I can picture her lying on her back, staring up at my stepfather and giggling as he sucked her toes and nuzzled his face in her tummy, her little arms reaching out to him. When he came home from work he poured himself a scotch on the rocks and put on the soundtrack from the movie *Butch Cassidy and the Sundance Kid.* He swept Kim up into his arms and the two of them danced to the song "Raindrops Keep Falling on My Head" on the walnut living room floor he had installed—part of the facelift he had given to our house after he married my mother. Once, a few years later, I put the soundtrack on without out thinking and watched the strange look of loss and longing fill my baby sister's face.

When my mother and stepfather came home from a night of drinking, they went upstairs to their bedroom, and from behind their shut door we heard loud breathing and moans that I later figured out were the sounds of lovemaking. More often than not they were too inebriated to hear the baby cry and one of my sisters or I would go in and pick Kim up and rock her back to sleep. If it was my turn I'd get out of bed in the pitch-black, put on my robe, and go downstairs to make her a bottle. I would have been eleven or twelve. My mother had taught me to heat up a saucepan with boiling water and then put the bottle filled with milk in the pan. She told me to test the temperature by pouring a drop of milk on the inside of my wrist to make sure it wasn't too hot for the baby. I'd go upstairs to the nursery, pick Kimmy up from her crib, and carry her over to the rocking chair to cradle her, enjoying the feel of her dense, damp body against mine. I'd feed her until the intoxication of the milk sealed her eyes shut.

Along with painstakingly picking out her layette, making sure everything was one hundred percent cotton, my mother bought a record of lullabies to play on a little turntable in Kim's room when we put her to sleep. *Bye bye baby bunting, Daddy's gone a hunting, to get a little rabbit skin to wrap his baby bunting in.* When I rocked her in my arms and kissed her, my lips would occasionally brush the warm peach fuzz on the top of her head and I'd take in her clean, milky, damp earth smell. All that mattered was the calmness of the night, my two other sisters asleep in their rooms, my mother and stepfather ensconced in theirs, and Kim snuggled against me, her little fingers wrapped around mine. The lullabies on the turntable eventually sent both of us to sleep. After my own son was born, I used to sing him the same lullabies when I put him to bed.

I liked to wake up in the morning and find my mother downstairs in the sunny kitchen, Kim sitting in her high chair while my mother spoon-fed her jars of applesauce and milky cereal. My mother had read somewhere that babies need to crawl to ensure strong eyesight. She was nervous that Kim, already pulling herself up, had never adequately learned, and she instructed my sisters and me to crawl on the floor to try and teach her. She insisted on cloth diapers instead of disposable ones. She taught me how to diaper Kim, how to stick the diaper pin in with my hand underneath the diaper so I wouldn't prick her, how to powder and bathe her, how to hold her properly by making sure to support her head because her neck wasn't yet strong enough. My mother took joy and pride in teaching us baby care. And taking care of the new baby gave her something to focus on when her husband was away on his endless business trips. He often said he'd be home on a certain day and then wouldn't get back until days later, which made her anxious and angry. Sometimes I'd see her pacing back and forth from the kitchen to the picture window in the living room waiting for his car to pull up. When he finally arrived, he'd come into the house, take Kim in his arms, and call her his baby girl. Her whole body came to attention and her little arms clung to his neck.

Looking back, I wonder if after five years of marriage he'd grown bored with the routine of family life. Or perhaps the passion between him and my mother was no longer alluring. I suppose he had experience with letting go. He had been married at least once before he married my mother. Sitting next to him on the couch, his solid body against me and his arm draped around my shoulder, I could sense his love. But there was another darker force inside him that could erupt at a moment's notice. I suspect he was afraid of getting too close to us or anyone. One morning my mother came down the stairs holding an icepack over a black eye. When we asked what happened, she told us that she'd tripped and fallen the night before. But remembering the shouting and the angry footsteps pacing back and forth upstairs that had gone on into the early hours of the morning, we weren't sure. Who knew what demons from his own childhood he endured? To us he was a man without a past who seemed to drop down on us from an alien planet.

When Kim was barely three, my mother discovered he'd been seeing someone else. Perhaps he got tired of the responsibilities of our family. The day he packed up his bags and left, remorseful and ashamed, he broke down and cried like a baby. When his eye caught mine I wanted to run to him and give him a hug, but in the end my loyalties lay with my mother. After he left she stayed in her room for days, upset and anxious, maybe wishing he'd come back to her and change his ways. When I'd sometimes bring Kim in to see her, she'd squeeze her daughter tighter than I'd ever seen her do before. I don't know whether there was ever an opportunity for my mother to have taken him back, or whether she would have. She was worn down by her desperate acts to please him. By the time Kim was three years old, the marriage was undeniably finished. My stepfather left and for ten years we never heard from him again.

BYE BYE BABY BUNTING

After my stepfather packed his clothes in his suitcase, took his rows of suits from the closet and his sweaters from the drawers, removed his shaving cream and razor from the bathroom, and left, we went back to being a house of women. At first, after she'd gotten over the agony of being left, my mother's decision to get a divorce empowered her. She was angry that her husband had treated her badly. Sometimes I would hear her cry herself to sleep in her bedroom and then get up in the morning and try to disguise her sadness. My darling daughters, she would say to us when she came downstairs. I think she felt she had failed us.

She tried to do a good job after my stepfather left. She gradually pulled herself together and began dating again. She left behind the scent of her expensive perfume when she went off in one man or another's car and came home with liquor on her breath. We sisters, as children do, fell into the new routine. After she left we would sit around and discuss each of our mother's dates, comparing and contrasting them, to figure out which one was the least offensive. The only one we liked was an intellectual of sorts, a pharmacist who took my mother to see foreign films at the art cinema at Cedar and Lee, but she preferred the ones more like our stepfather who liked to drink and have a good time. We sisters took care of Kim while our mother went on dates. We were live-in babysitters. Sometimes we'd all pile into my mother's king-size bed, with Kim in the middle, and watch *The Patty Duke Show* or *Gilligan's Island* on TV. We pretended the bed was a boat and we were held captive at sea. *There were four in the bed, and the little one said, roll over, roll over, so we all rolled over and one fell out, there were three in the bed and the little one said* . . .

When I wasn't at school, I spent my days reading novels in my bedroom, infatuated with Heathcliff and Mr. Darcy, relating my fatherless self to Jane Eyre and David Copperfield, and wishing to be as strong and serious as Jo in *Little Women.* I wrote long entries in my diary, rode my bike around the neighborhood, and spread my beach blanket on the lawn beside my friends at the neighborhood pool. But because of my father's early death, a part of me felt separate from my friends, as if I alone knew the world of disruption and grief. Babysitting for Kim helped stave off the loneliness and estrangement of adolescence. She was such an easy baby. She liked to sit on the floor and play quietly with her dollhouse or ride her pink tricycle up and down the block. She enjoyed tea parties, pouring invisible cups of tea from her china tea set for her teddy bears. There was nothing I liked more than hearing her call out my name. She loved Big Bird and Oscar the Grouch and laughed at the Cookie Monster on *Sesame Street.* She liked to hop on my lap with *The Lonely Doll* or *Red Fish, Blue Fish* so I could read to her. While she listened, she twirled a strand of my long hair around her finger. Occasionally I would look up and stare at the empty black leather Eames chair sitting in the living room. The chair was a reminder that Kim had not been miraculously conceived. I held her closer to me as if I could make up for what she had lost.

Even as a teenager I guessed there would be repercussions for Kim once her father had left. I suppose I thought we older sisters could make up for some of it. We were fatherless, too.

––––––––––

On one of my visits to Cleveland when my son was young, I took him to the playground at the elementary school we had all attended. It was three blocks away from our house. When I babysat Kim I used to take her to that playground. Imagine a newborn baby and an awkward and shy thirteen-year-old girl hungry for love. We bonded intensely. Remarkably, one of my friends, also the middle child in a family of three, had a little sister the same age as Kim. We pushed our little sisters in our strollers side by side on the sidewalk to the schoolyard as if we were young mothers. We sat on the concrete wall of the sandbox, our bottoms getting cold and damp as we talked about school or boys or whatever young girls talked about, while our little sisters dug invisible tunnels with their shovels. We pushed them on the swings, wiped dirt from their hands, and picked them up when they fell. Years later, when I took Lucas to the same playground and watched him playing in the sandbox and climbing on the jungle gym, I saw in my mind the phantom of Kim, squealing as she raced down the slide.

PLAYING HOUSE

We sisters rallied to help my mother with Kim now that she was a single mother again. My mother used to boast that Kim had four mothers. We gave Kim elaborate birthday parties in our kitchen and invited her friends from the neighborhood. We blew up the colored balloons and tied them to each child's chair, served the Big Bird birthday cake, blindfolded the children for Pin the Tail on the Donkey, making sure that Kim would win. Even though we were Jewish, every year we put up a Christmas tree, a tradition that had started when my mother married my stepfather. We would go with my mother to the nursery to pick out the tree and lug it from the car to our living room, leaving a trail of pine needles in our wake. There was something slightly subversive about it—Jews with a Christmas tree. But our mother didn't want to disappoint us. Sometimes we had to string the lights around the tree two or three times before we managed to get them right. Proud of the spectacle we'd created, we adorned the tree with necklaces of popcorn, cranberries, and tinsel and boosted Kim up so she could crown the miracle with a white satin angel to protect us from harm. On the night before Christmas, we took Kim downtown to Higbee's department store to see Santa. Dressed in her blue snowsuit with white fur around the hood, she perched in Santa's lap squirming to get away, barely waiting for the photographer to snap her picture. But the real magic of Christmas came in watching Kim walk down the stairs in the morning, dancing on her tiptoes with excitement when she saw the filled stockings hanging from the mantel and the wrapped presents under the Christmas tree. One year my mother bought her a dollhouse with miniature wood furniture, chintz curtains, little made-up beds, and a perfect family of carved dolls, father dressed in his suit, mother with an apron around her waist, two sisters and a brother, as if to create what we lacked. Kim spent hours sitting in front of the dollhouse, moving the little family figures around from room to room, locked away in a secret fantasy. Once she broke down in tears because she couldn't find the miniature father doll. We searched underneath the cushions of the furniture and around the floor until we found him.

One summer, Cindy and I, fourteen and fifteen, set up a small camp at our house to make extra money. We had seven or eight toddlers from the neighborhood; Kim, with her hair in pigtails and a space in the middle of her smile where she'd lost a baby tooth, was our favorite camper. In the mornings we played Duck Duck Goose, Red Rover, and What Time Is It Mr. Fox on the front lawn. On the picnic table we concocted art projects: little treasure boxes with glued-on sequins that stuck to our damp skin or log cabins out of Popsicle sticks. We ran the sprinkler in the backyard and filled up the baby pool. Kim sometimes grew jealous if we gave too much attention to another camper in the group. She was possessive of her older sisters. Once she went inside to go to the bathroom and ran back out of the house overly excited to return, afraid of what she'd been missing, fell down on the stone walk, and cut her head. Blood gushed from her forehead. We took her to the emergency room and while she got stitched up I held her hand. She stared up at me and our eyes locked. She did not cry once.

But Christmas, birthday parties, and summer camp were no substitute for a father's presence. His leaving created a river of longing beginning the day he left the house when she was three years old and not seeing her again until she was thirteen. *Bye bye baby bunting, Daddy's gone a hunting. To get a little rabbit skin to wrap his baby bunting in.* It was hard not to feel that we'd done something to fail him. I'm sure Kim thought so, too.

RUNAWAY

My mother sent Kim to sleep-away camp in southern Ohio with her two best friends the summer before she was going into fifth grade. This is the first letter she sent home:

> *Dear Mom,*
>
> > *How are you? I'm having a great time at camp. I hate swimming though. Please write me. I think I like riding the best. The people in my cabin are nice. How's Leo* [a kitten Cindy brought home] *Gretel and Jill? The foods terrible and they don't give you enough to eat. My trunk is so messy. I have to go riding. Bye. Love, Kim*
> >
> > *P.S. I love you*

But a few days later my mother received this note on the same stationery with two little calico dogs dipping their paws into ink in the corner of the paper:

> *Dear Mom,*
>
> > *I miss you. I hate it here. I am always crying cause I miss you. Please call me and say its an emergency because it is. I can't stand it here. If you don't call by Wed at 1:00 I'm running away from camp.*
> >
> > *From Kim*

My mother called the camp director, and she let Kim talk to her. "I can't, mommy, I can't," my mother told us Kim repeated, crying uncontrollably, unable to calm herself down. My mother was beside herself with worry. She wanted to drive to the camp and bring Kim home that evening, but the camp director persuaded her not to. After the phone call my mother was anxious and inconsolable. She said there was something in Kim's voice beyond the range of homesickness that many children experience being away from home for the first time. "A mother knows," she said, irritated that we challenged her. Later that night in the pitch-black darkness of the country, Kim, only nine years old, escaped from the camp using a flashlight to guide her and walked a mile down the rocky pebble-strewn road until she came to a stranger's house. She knocked on the door and asked the owner of the house if she could call my mother. My mother then called the camp director, angry that they'd let Kim wander away unattended. The director brought Kim back to the camp and kept her there until we arrived to collect her the next day.

To this day my mother talks about the tenacity Kim possessed. "You could never tell her what to do once she set her mind on something." My mother believed Kim's fear of separation had to do with an unconscious response to her father's loss. I did, too. I wrote this poem not long after Kim ended her life.

The Runaway

On a summer day full of promise
we piled into my mother's car
and drove my youngest sister
to camp for the summer.

That night she ran away
and called from a stranger's
house to beg our mother
to bring her home.

Years later,
she took the keys
to my mother's white Saab,
closed the garage door
and turned on the ignition.

On a day less remembered
for the violent rain
than for how little was the same as before,
the sky closed its eyes on our house
as if in shame and claimed her.

SISTERS

We older sisters traipsed in and out of the house with our friends or shut ourselves away in our bedrooms, listening to Neil Young on the record player. It was the mid-seventies. We went to keg parties, smoked marijuana, and got stoned on quaaludes. We slammed doors and fought with each other and with our mother. Kim stole our makeup and cigarettes, read our strange books about Eastern philosophy written by maharajahs from India or obscure Chinese poets. She and her girlfriends spied on us when we snuck our boyfriends into the house after our mother had gone to bed. My high school boyfriend flirted with her by sometimes chasing her through the house or tackling her on the front lawn. We drove her and two or three close friends she had known since preschool to the movies or the mall, or took them out for pizza. Growing up with three teenage girls at home must have created a dark, rich, emotionally charged world for a child. This is something Kim wrote on a tablet of lined paper in big block letters when she was a kid:

> *I wish I had a dog so I would have someone to play with.*
> *I wish I was 21 so I could order my sisters.*
> *I wish I had a big room so I could have more people over.*

Sometimes it must have been too much, my mother anxious and falling into long periods of melancholy, Cindy a little too wild, Laura drifting into private solitude, and me prone to moodiness. I wondered if Kim sensed the chaotic fragility of our lives, with no one sturdy to anchor us. The sight of my boyfriend when he came to fetch me in his faded jeans, tight T-shirt, and broad shoulders filled my body with intensity and excitement. I tried not to lose myself in my infatuation, but being with him took me away from the cloud of uncertainty and unrest at home. Like all teenagers, I was embarrassed by my mother and afraid of what others would intuit of the mysteries and secrets within my family. I worried that Kim would pick up on my weakness. I tried to be cheerful and give the impression that I was strong. I knew she relied on my sisters and me as role models and to provide her with a sense of her self-worth. How strange it must have been when one by one we left home. *There were four in the bed and the little one said, roll over, roll over, so we all rolled over and one fell out.* My older sister, Laura, moved to California. A year later, after working summer jobs and cashing in my savings, I went to college. A year after that, Cindy did, too. By the time Kim was ten she was like an only child.

I returned home on long weekends and holidays to visit (I went to Ohio University in Athens, Ohio, three hours away), and when Kim heard the car pull up the driveway she ran outside to greet me with her blond hair streaming behind her and fell into my arms. When I looked at the house from the driveway, unease snaked inside me. That feeling has followed me to this day.

I don't want to think about the nights Kim was left with a babysitter while my mother went out, or think about her watching, as we did when we were her age, as my mother obsessively prepared herself for her dates so she could walk down the stairs more confidently. I don't want to imagine how Kim felt the nights my mother might have come home in the early hours of the morning. I don't want to think she worried about my mother, as I did when I was her age. Even then I feared for Kim's fate and was looking for reasons for her to "survive the night." This is a poem I wrote for her when I was in my first year of graduate school and Kim was twelve, my first published work, about the journey through adolescence. After Kim died our beloved aunt Harriet typed the poem on white paper and insisted we bury it with Kim inside her casket.

Sisters

Opening the door I expect to find you there
tripping the steps, thin wing of hair
sweeping behind, the color of half-ripened corn.

A welcome one dreams about, coming home from the seas or war.
This time I see you have changed.
Upstairs harboring behind our door

the way we hid together behind books,
entered worlds we hadn't known, prairies we stumbled across,
little women, petticoats, herbal recipes,

secret gardens we believed were real, red barns,
horses that could make you cry, magic, painted roads.
The dark at the end of the forest sweating in your dreams.

Now inside your room parcels of childhood
arrange themselves like down quilted on your bed,
I carry them in my arms while you pull away.

I'm surprised finding your face thinned, diamond white,
eyes that pool tears so much like stars, the light behind them.
Your hair, like fallen leaves, dies a little more each day;

the color is a suspension of yellow and brown.
Your small breasts float on your chest, are apple blossoms
bobbing in a pond. Your body wanders off like a shadow.

It all comes back, hurrying past every mirror,
giving in to that last trail of light, then in bed suspending
that moment in dreams of yourself, women you flip in magazines.

I want to make it all easy, or at least have answers
for the old body shed, for the new horrors
that arise at night, for parents quarreling,

for friends turning away and returning daily,
for desires you can't name, longings for the ease of a dream,
answers I can't give you. Reasons for surviving the night.

REUNION

When Kim was thirteen, she began asking about her father. The only time my mother talked about him with us older girls was when she was embattled with him over child support and alimony. I'm not sure what she said privately to Kim about her father. What did Kim tell her friends or her teachers when they asked about him? In grade school I was embarrassed when the topic of fathers came up. Once we were making Father's Day cards and I was pulled aside and told to make a card for my grandfather. I would have preferred to make a card for my own father—didn't my teacher know he was still alive inside for me, my secret protection? But for Kim, what kind of an explanation would there be for why her father didn't see her? I don't know how much my mother ever explained to Kim. I don't remember talking much about it to her, though I wondered how Kim felt when her father, who used to lift her up and squeeze her when he came home, was no longer there. When she began to walk, before he left, she used to slip her tiny feet into his inflexible black shoes.

When Kim began asking about her father, my mother went to see a psychologist for advice, and the psychologist encouraged her to contact Kim's father so that Kim could establish her own relationship with him. My mother wasn't sure about it. To this day she wonders whether she should have. She didn't know what kind of effect seeing him would have on Kim or how he would treat her. Out of all of us, she knew him best, but even she didn't know how to explain to her daughter that he'd been living on the west side of Cleveland during the years when she learned her alphabet, was in her grade school plays, learned to ride her first bike. Persuaded by the psychologist's advice that Kim would have to find out who he was for herself, my mother broke the decade of silence and called him.

He drove up to our house in a fancy town car with armloads of presents for Kim—much like he had done for our mother when he took her on a shopping spree and once for us girls before school started—and took her away with him for a weekend. When he came through the front door to pick her up I stayed in my bedroom, holding my breath, a little sick inside, not certain what to do. For Kim's sake I finally went out to greet him. I was a young woman then, in college. He remarked how grown up I was, and we smiled the awkward smile of two people who once shared an affection but understood that a vast gap had grown between them. Once he left the house with Kim, I peeked out the shutters in my bedroom and watched Kim get into the car, as I once had at her age, and felt a strange combination of envy and protectiveness. When Kim returned home she was on cloud nine. Perhaps he draped his arm over her shoulder. I love you, sweetheart, he might have said. She was beaming as if a light inside her that had been shut off had been switched back on. She announced that her father was going to redecorate our house. The house had grown shabby during the years since he had left. The new couches that he had bought for our living room were faded and there were rips in the cushions. The paint on the outside of the house was peeling and the bushes were overgrown. I have no doubt that at the time her father said he was going to fix up our house, he meant it. He liked for things to look good. Perhaps he felt guilty seeing that our house had begun to show signs of wear and tear inside and out. I'm sure it bothered him to think of his youngest daughter living in a state of disrepair. But after he closed his car door and pulled out of the driveway and left, the loose pebbles from the drive kicking into his tires, no doubt his good intentions receded, too. Kim spoke of him with stars in her eyes. She was in love.

That courtship lasted a year or two. He picked her up once every few months and took her for the weekend, sometimes with her best friend, Mary, to a place he had on a small island on the lake. He had an on-top-of-the-world smile, wore khaki pants and emerald polo shirts, exuded a carefree, withholding kind of air. He was always tan. Kim said they went motor boating and sailing and out to expensive dinners where the adults partied and drank. He was the kind of man who could seduce a person with his smile and his infectious laughter. He liked to have a good time, and liked for the people around him to have fun, too. He was like a towering building in front of which a young girl cranes her neck to take in the sight. And yet there was a disconnect between what he seemed to be and what he was capable of doing.

Not long after they'd begun seeing each other, her father soon began to find fault with her. He didn't like the way she dressed. He wanted her to wear Lacoste shirts and Docksiders instead of blue jeans and peasant shirts. He saw things in black and white; she was more dreamy and ethereal. Kim told me that on one of her weekends away with her father he teased his oldest daughter, then in her early twenties, because she had gained weight. I think what worried Kim was the fear that the way he treated his eldest daughter was a harbinger of what was to come for her. I sensed Kim was disappointed that he didn't spend a lot of time with her. I don't think she ever got over his desertion or ever believed in the security of his affection. But she was protective of him, too. She rarely talked about him. In her silences resided the pit of her love. Sometimes I would find her alone in her room with photos from their time at the lake in her hand.

I know what it is like to grow up without a father. A daughter never stops longing for the kind of love she imagines a father could provide. But what if the father is alive? That single factor is what separated my youngest sister from us three older girls. Our father was dead; hers was among the living.

BLACK STONES

I write this narrative for months, probing my childhood years and re-creating a portrait of Kim to connect the dots. While I am writing, it is as though Kim has morphed into a presence guiding my fingers on the keyboard, telling me what is permissible to say. One memory unlocks another and I am reassured by remembering the precious little girl she was and how much she was loved. And then I am stricken by what we missed. I work for an hour or two each morning and then I go to work and Kim is still with me, next to me on the subway. Back at home she watches me cook dinner. She gets to know my son and I like having her with me, this phantom self, and I think she is living her life through me and I am comforted by her presence.

When I go out to our house near the beach I take a walk along the ocean and decide to collect only black stones. They are my worry stones. I have private conversations with Kim on the beach. I am thinking about you, I say to her. Can you hear me?

THE HOUSE OF WOMEN

I worried about leaving my mother and Kim alone together in our white house half-buried by overgrown shrubs, but I had been preparing to go to college for years and didn't know what else might be an option. I babysat when I was thirteen, at sixteen worked in a bakery after school and on weekends, and then took up waitressing to save money. All of us girls could chart our teenage years from the places we worked: the bakery counter of Hough Bakery; Sand's Deli, which in the early eighties turned into a disco at night; Baskin Robbins; the counter of a greasy spoon on Chagrin and Lee; and Geraci's pizza parlor.

If I didn't go to college and make something of myself I feared that my mother's dependent predicament would be my fate (the same way I later worried that I might be plagued by depression), as if it had been imprinted in my genetic makeup. I worked determinedly—all of us girls did—to save enough money to put myself through college. I put my tips in the top drawer of my closet and at night counted every nickel, dime, and penny. My mother hadn't any extra money to help me. I didn't mind working. I liked the orderliness of wiping down the counter and tables, filling up the salt shakers and ketchup bottles for the following day. When we closed the restaurant, I sprayed the glass cabinets with Windex and counted the

cash by putting the bills into rubber-banded denominations;
I liked the busy work of balancing the day's expenses. Against
the disorder of my home life, the workplace was a temple of
serenity—the daily routine, small talk with the customers, the
satisfaction of knowing my boss approved of my work. I used
to say to myself, if all else fails at least I could do this one thing.

During my last years of high school my mother worried obsessively about money, and her worry penetrated the rest of us
like the dampness after a long rain. We saw that she was most
alive when there was a new man in her life—and the potential for happiness and a comfortable future that the new man
would surely bestow. But with that came the other message she
inadvertently left us with: that without a man she was nothing.
And therefore neither were we. She often slipped in and out
of melancholy, as she had before she married my stepfather.
The anxiety and fear of being alone, without financial security,
combined with her severe migraines, would take her to her
bedroom where she would pull down the blinds and stay in
bed sometimes all day until the headache lifted.

When her spirits were good, my mother was a different person.
I loved watching her prepare to entertain for Christmas dinner, the only time she entertained at our house. For weeks she
scoured cookbooks and magazines until she put together the
perfect menu. Once she compiled her grocery list she began two
or three days of shopping, searching for the freshest vegetables
and best cuts of meat, the butteriest baked goods. When she
came home she arranged her ingredients on the kitchen coun-

ters and then, throughout the days that followed, gave each of her girls a job. Only the perfect salad dressing would do, only the most appetizing presentation would please her. If her famous whipped strawberry Jell-O mold refused to mold to her satisfaction, she chucked it into the sink and began all over again. The lesson was simple. Given the liberty to be creative, my mother was a master of the domestic arts. It was the fundamental skills of learning a living or trade in the world that confounded her.

I fantasized that once my other two sisters and I were out of the house and her worry about us alleviated, my mother could focus more energy on her own life and on Kim's. And I know that she tried. Still, I sensed that no matter how much I wished my mother would pull her life together, there was something that seemed to keep her from it. I noticed when I came home for visits from college, guilty for having left them, that she was relying on Kim to help her if she couldn't get the car started or if the basement flooded or if the furnace kicked off. The smallest things could undo her. She liked to boast that Kim knew how to do everything. She counted on Kim for companionship. And Kim counted on her.

Happy Birthday, to a wonderful mother and my great friend, Kim wrote one year inside a birthday card with a sketch of a cat on the front of it that looked exactly like Gretel. *You're the best mom in the world,* said another. The two of them sometimes ate takeout together or watched a movie on TV. Other nights, my mother spent her evenings alone upstairs in her bedroom reading the newspaper, watching television, doing crossword puzzles, or occasionally circling help-wanted ads in the paper, as she had done when I lived at home.

Downstairs, Kim made a teenage fortress of her bedroom, her books and papers strewn across her bed, where she did her homework or daydreamed. With the tenderness in her breasts, the cramping like a knot waiting to unwind in her abdomen, the confused swirl of hormones, and the incessant longing to be kissed, she, like most adolescent girls, grew more secretive. She smiled with her lips over her teeth to cover her braces and pulled at her T-shirts and sweaters to hide her changing body, though within a matter of months it had evened out into a beautiful figure. Her hair, once fine and silky, had grown thicker and longer. I occasionally saw her glancing at herself in the mirror with a look of bewilderment.

My mother, disappointed by her own situation and worried about her daughters and her future, uncertain of what to do, gradually retreated into her own private world. She often needed pills to get herself going in the morning and another pill to fall asleep at night. Her daughters were her pride and joy. When I went away to college—she herself having left college after one semester to get married—she remarked that I was doing what she had never finished. In the scar of her smile I intuited all that she'd lost. If one of us was upset because our boyfriend didn't call, or we'd been dumped, my mother mourned with us. "You can't trust him," she used to say, as if to convince herself. "We don't need them, darling." But nevertheless, we grew up thinking our lives rose and fell depending on how a person of the opposite sex viewed us, whether that meant our absent fathers or the boys we gave our hearts to.

In our house of women, men were our enemies and also our saviors. We looked up to their cool strong bodies and their impenetrable eyes; we were enamored by their capable hands and their aloof smiles; we wanted to possess their sense of freedom and daring. We thought they might be safe houses in which to store our wounded hearts. We were wrong.

THE SNOWMAN

It is winter now. My thirteenth winter with Lucas. Only one snowfall this year. I am in the country, standing on our deck overlooking the yard. The snow has frozen over the field of grass. I don't know why I have a vision of Kim when she was a little girl dressed in her light blue snowsuit with the little trim of white fur around her hood. On the day I am remembering it is morning in Cleveland and it has snowed all night. When we wake up the house is cold and we can hear the kick of the furnace turning on. Outside snow is everywhere, on the shrubs and trees, against the front door, piled up twelve inches high. Kim is excited and wants to go out and walk in it. I am fifteen and she is five. When we leave the house it seems we are the only people in the universe. The snow goes up to her waist, and when she walks she falls and begins to laugh. We make a snowman, rolling the first ball across the lawn while it builds in girth and strength as if we are rolling a wheel up a hill. Kim's cheeks are rosy. Many times she falls and we always laugh. Then we roll the second ball, then the third, ransacking the snow-filled lawn. What thrills her most is when it is time to make the face. She likes giving the snowman a carrot nose, a mouth made of raisins from the little box of Sunkist in her pocket. Since we have no men in the house and hence no top hat, we give our snowman a stocking cap and for some reason this delights her. Oh winter, I think, oh ice, oh frozen memories thawing like the snow on top of the awning underneath which I sit watching my husband and son throw a football on the white torn-up lawn.

part three

EVIDENCE

During Lucas's babyhood I tried to stay focused on the present. Lucas was an active, engaging baby, always throwing out his arms and kicking his legs with excitement; he consumed our world. On the weekends I'd sometimes bundle him up in his fleece jacket, put him in a snuggly, and meet a friend for coffee. But I had trouble concentrating on adult conversation. Every thought and neuron was tuned to Lucas. I knew it was not uncommon for mothers, and no different for adoptive mothers, to feel this way, but I also wondered whether my fierce attachment and anxiety had to do with the fear of something bad happening to him. It had happened before.

In moments when I should have been happy, I sometimes fretted. At times, in secret, I succumbed to periods where I wanted to spend mornings sleeping, or lingering in the bedroom, sometimes almost paralyzed by a heaviness and mysterious fatigue that would not lift. At times I viewed the world darkly; isolated and consumed by a sense of foreboding, I thought that only those who had experienced the loss of a loved one by suicide could understand. During those periods it was as if I was only going through the motions of living.

Throughout the years that I was consumed with trying

to have a baby, and then with being a young mother, to keep myself from sliding I tried not to dwell on Kim or the emotional pain that led to her suicide. But memories of her surfaced against my will. Changing Lucas's diaper, I remembered the time I had accidentally pricked Kim with a diaper pin and how fearful I had been, certain I had harmed her. I remembered the moment I slipped down the stairs with her cradled in my arms and for weeks afterward was consumed by the thought that I might have seriously injured her.

I dreamed about her as an infant or a little girl, sometimes visceral, colorful dreams in which she was with me again, wearing her yellow nightgown that clung to her body, her clear unblemished face crowned by soft, baby-fine blond hair. Always at the end of the dream she'd be calling out for me and I couldn't reach her. Or I would find myself writing about her, first in my poems and then later in an essay that would become the impetus for this book. When I was writing, the connections began to come together and miraculously I felt I was bringing her back to life.

When I was desperate for answers, reading whatever I could get my hands on about suicide—philosophical, sociological, or psychological studies—I found myself longing for the story of the individual soul. Where was the story of the young girl who brightened over the simple pleasures of a box of animal crackers or a piggyback ride, who loved cats and playing hide and seek, who possessed the gift of generosity and had held such promise? I could catch glimpses of her in the language of despair written by poets or in works of fiction. But it wasn't enough. I could find no full portrait of a living, breathing human being, no different from any one of us, who had lost the will to live.

It bothered me when I heard in passing a suicide dismissed as someone who was messed up or crazy, as if each person was unaffected by others who share and shape the world around him or her. I thought of John Donne's famous lines:

> No man is an island, entire of itself;
> Every man is a piece of the continent,
> A part of the main.

I was especially dismayed when people cast blame or faulted Kim for taking her life. I also became more sensitive to this tendency when anyone spoke of a suicide; even in her death, I wanted to protect Kim from that kind of ridicule or shame. When her name was mentioned sometimes among extended family or friends, silence ensued. Would her memory always be diminished and sullied by suicide? It also upset me when people assumed because she'd committed suicide that she had been depressed. It seemed dismissive. Some psychologists believe suicide is not directly linked to depression.

Through words, I began to piece Kim's life together, trying to articulate the forces that undermined her sense of self and to restore her dignity. For a time this work kept at bay the internal chaos her suicide provoked inside me. I wanted to bring her back, to change the course of what had happened. This was my war with myself. I felt I had two impossible options: If I didn't accept her death, then it would be as if she hadn't died and left us. If I could make sense of what happened and grasp it, through writing about her, maybe I could let her go.

The morning of June 16, 1998, eight years after Kim died and three years after Lucas was born, I finally decided to obtain concrete answers. I found that when I was actively engaged in attempting to understand her suicide, the heaviness I carried abated a little. There was a part of me that hoped Kim hadn't wanted to die, and sometimes, not being able to fathom what she'd done, I tricked myself into thinking that what happened was an accident or that she'd been drugged or even murdered. From my phone at home (I took notes and kept them in a file in my desk drawer) I called the high school she'd attended to see if I could find a record of what went wrong at school and why the administration had permitted her to drop out only a few months short of her diploma. I asked the school to send me a copy of her records, but after being put on hold and transferred from one person to another, I was told that the records were not available. Perhaps the administration was fearful of a lawsuit.

Next I called the police department. The officer on duty explained that I needed to send in a written request for the police report. He said he was willing to help. Tears filled my eyes. Again, it was this magical idea that had taken possession of me: if I found out exactly what happened, Kim would be redeemed, maybe return, and in this particular drama the officer was my accomplice. He understood my need for evidence. I suppose that, being in that job, he had come across unspeakable family tragedies before. He explained how I could get a copy of the autopsy report and directed me to the Cuyahoga County coroner's office. I don't know what I expected to find. Some specific clue as to what sent Kim into the car that night and made her shut the garage door in the darkness? A week or so later an envelope from the police department landed in my mailbox. I brought the envelope into my apartment, afraid of what I would find inside. On top of the photocopied paper was her case number: #206531. The autopsy report shared the same number. I read the first page of the report over several times, unable to take it in:

At 1010 hrs. on 4/16/90 I responded to [address] in reference to an automobile with its engine running inside a detached garage with the garage door closed. When I arrived, neighbors had already raised the garage door. The garage was full of smoke from the exhaust and I could see what appeared to be a female slumped down in the front passenger seat with her head leaning against the side window. I attempted to open the passenger door but it was locked. I then went around to the driver's door which was unlocked and its window rolled down. I got into the auto and backed it out of the garage and turned the ignition off. Shaker Hts. Rescue squad personnel arrived and could detect no signs of life. Cpl. [officer's name] notified the coroner's office at 1050 hrs and spoke to intake officer [officer's name].

Lake Ambulance responded, unit 555 with OIV's [officer's name] and the body was removed from the auto and taken to the coroner's office.

At 1230 hrs. I contacted the coroner's office and spoke to [doctor's name] who advised me that [doctor's name] pronounced the body at 1134 hrs. preliminary indications for cause of death—asphyxiation by carbon monoxide poisoning.

What was she wearing? There was no mention of it on the page. It was as if the report could have been about any girl found dead in a car. As I tried to make out the words, often rendered obscure by the faintness of the photocopy, sadness overcame me. I stuffed the report back into the envelope. I couldn't read any more.

EVIDENCE II

For days I refused to read the second page of the report written by officers, dated 04/16/90, time: 1010. It was one thing to digest that Kim had ended her life by her own hand and to accept her suffering, but it was another to read the facts written up by a stranger. At home at my desk, my eyes repeatedly sought out the folder where I kept the report. I was unable to tell anyone about it. I was afraid others would wonder why, after so many years, I still hadn't come to terms with Kim's suicide. Yet what did that even mean? Coming to terms? Closure? Acceptance? I did not believe I would ever be able to accept it. A few days later I braced myself, and when I was home alone I took out the folder and read the rest of the report.

[Kim's mother] was awakened by S.H.P.D at 1030 this morning.

She stated her daughter had been feeling very depressed ever since October but didn't know if the problem was a boyfriend or something else. [Kim's mother] wanted her daughter to get some counseling but she couldn't get Kim to see anyone.

Victim was found slumped in the front passenger seat of the listed auto wearing a dark blue sweat suit, no jewelry.

A suicide note, written on a yellow legal pad and identified by [her mother] as her daughter's handwriting was found on a chair in the kitchen. The original suicide note is attached to this report and copies of the note along with photos taken by PTL. [officer's name] were placed in Evidence Locker T-8.

At 1330 hrs. I contacted OIV [one of Kim's friend's] who stated that she picked up victim Kim at her residence at

2030 hrs., she states Kim did not speak of hurting herself and the fight that Kim was involved in with her ex-boyfriend, Alan, occurred over the phone. [Kim's friend] states she left the Colony Lounge at 2300 hours.

I attempted to contact Ex-Boyfriend Alan but got no answer.

The vehicle [Kim] was found in had been parked in the garage earlier in the day by OIV [her mother].

It was those simple things—no jewelry—blue sweatshirt and sweatpants—suicide note—that made it palpable. After the shock of reading the words on the page, I found an odd comfort in seeing manifest the facts of how she had been found, the care the police officers had taken to get down the details, perhaps because everything else about her suicide was amorphous and intangible. But it opened up other questions. How had she gathered up the courage? Why that night? How had she known what to do? She must have thought about suicide a lot, I presumed.

EVIDENCE III

The Report of Toxicology findings indicated that the substances in her body at the time of death were cocaine and benzodiazepines. When I Googled the effect of the combination of those two drugs, I read that sometimes benzodiazepines are used to relieve the side effects, irritability and agitation, associated with cocaine binges. I had known that she had been drinking that night, and I suspected that she had also been using drugs. Now another piece of the puzzle was confirmed. I took comfort in the thought that the euphoric effects of the drugs might have lessened her searing emotional pain, but whatever comfort that had granted quickly disappeared. Had the drugs exacerbated her sense of hopelessness and pushed her over the edge? I read that substance abuse can decrease one's judgment and increase impulsivity. And how had she gotten to the point where she felt there was no hope?

TALKING TO THE DEAD

The more I know, the more I can bear. My mother is the opposite. She has never seen the police or autopsy report, nor does she want to. She has not been to my sister's grave since the day Kim was buried, when we could not pry her away from the ground beside her daughter's plot. Kim is always with her. Every day my mother talks to her youngest daughter. She often shares it with me. "Aunt Harriet's with Kimmy now," she said, just a month or two ago, the moment she learned Aunt Harriet had died. "Kim would have liked that sweater." "It was Kimmy's favorite," if we were eating pizza from Geraci's. "I fixed the dryer. Kim told me how to do it." On Kim's birthday she calls me to remember the event together. We light a Yahrzeit candle on the anniversary of her death every year. My mother puts the candle in the sink, perhaps afraid that the rage of God for forsaking a child will set the house on fire. She believes that her daughter was in agony and that she chose not to suffer; she needs to believe that through her death Kim now lives on a higher plane. "Why else are flowers so beautiful?"

she says to me. "Why is the sky such a perfect shade of blue? There has to be more than the here and now."

FATE IS LIKE A BIRD

Having digested the facts revealed in the police and autopsy reports—there seemed now no question in my mind about what Kim had done—I continued to read everything I could about suicide. I looked for overlays between what I read and what I knew about Kim. My research drew me to Dr. Edwin Shneidman's influential book, *The Suicidal Mind,* published in 1998. Shneidman, a leading expert on suicide, founded the Los Angeles Suicide Prevention Center with his colleagues Dr. Robert Littman and Dr. Norman Farberow. Shneidman developed a program in suicide prevention for the National Institute of Mental Health and has published a score of books on suicide; he also wrote the essay on suicide for the 1973 edition of the *Encyclopædia Britannica*. He coined the term "suicidology" and founded the American Association of Suicidology, an organization devoted to research on suicide. In his early work, he and Farberow conducted a large study that contradicted some widely held beliefs about suicide. For example, although it had long been thought that people had to be insane to take their own lives, they found that only 15 percent of suicides were psychotic. They also developed the idea that those people who are acutely suicidal are only in that state for a short period of time and that intervention is essential. For some reason, the idea that Kim may have been suicidal only for a short period of time gave me comfort. It confirmed what I'd felt, that in those

last months Kim may have been fighting for her life and that
her strength during those last hours, perhaps even moments,
had defeated her. Shneidman believes suicide is the result of an
interior dialogue. The mind scans its available options until it
accepts suicide as a solution.

In *The Suicidal Mind,* Shneidman argues that the suicidal
individual suffers from "psychache," "the hurt, anguish or ache
that takes hold in the mind," and that the catalyst for a suicide
is psychological pain.

> Even though I know that each suicidal death is a mul-
> tifaceted event—that biological, biochemical, cultural, so-
> ciological, interpersonal, intrapsychic, logical, philosophical,
> conscious, and unconscious elements are always present—I
> retain the belief that, in the proper distillation of the event,
> its essential nature is psychological. That is, each suicidal
> drama occurs in the mind of a unique individual.

Suicide raises epistemological, philosophical, and spiritual
questions. Some accounts suggest that it is caused by differences and problems in the brain and emotions, and that
chemicals such as serotonin are not found in the same levels in
suicides. Mental illness and depression may be evident, and research has found genetic patterns at the root of many suicides.
But what all suicides have in common is mental pain.

The vulnerability of the mind is what Shneidman and researchers like him have spent their lives trying to uncover. In
the culture at large there is a tendency to biologize suicide,
make it a psychiatric disease called depression and treat it with

medication. Shneidman's position is to recognize the mental pain.

The psychological aspects related to the suicidal act were revealed to Shneidman and his colleagues through what they call a "psychological autopsy," which is a psychological reconstruction of the intentions of the deceased. This reconstruction is based on information collected from personal documents, police reports, medical and coroner's records, and interviews with families, friends, and others who had contact with the person before their death. They designed this form of autopsy to determine the cause of death in cases where the mode of death is uncertain. It also addresses the question "why?"

Reading Shneidman's perspective on suicide seemed to ease, at least during the moments I read and reflected on his work, some of the confusion I felt about what made Kim take her life. Before I read his work, I believed that a person could learn how to surround herself with an imaginary wall as a form of protection against the horrors and tragic losses and separations that the passage of time inflicts on us. But I did not fully understand that individuals are not always the authors of themselves, especially at the age of nineteen, twenty, or twenty-one. Some, more sensitive, cannot arm themselves with the necessary skills to find work or pursue an education; and when the pain is all-consuming, they cannot build a wall of protection. Phrased another way, perhaps not all of us are able to survive natural selection, a struggle for life in which only those organisms best adapted to existing conditions are able to survive and reproduce. Suicides remind us of our vulnerability.

After reading Shneidman's work I was curious about the psychological autopsy he described. For the "autopsy" the psychologist interviews those close to the deceased to try to reconstruct their last days. I wondered if such an autopsy would help me understand what had happened to Kim.

Then one day over lunch, by chance, through my work as an editor, I met Shneidman's literary agent. She gave me his address. I wrote this letter to him.

September 8, 2000
Dear Edwin Shneidman:

I had lunch a few months ago with your agent. I did not know at the time that she was your agent and I felt it was by some stroke of coincidence and luck that we should meet. Let me explain. Along with being an editor, I am also a poet and writer. I have been working on a book about my sister's suicide that I am calling *History of a Suicide*. In an essay that will form part of this book, I have cited your work.

I think you have done more than any one writer I have read, aside from the great poets and philosophers, in furthering the understanding of suicide in this country. I am writing to ask whether you would be willing to do a psychological autopsy of my sister. . . . What I would like to emphasize in my book is that suicide does not happen in a vacuum. I want to record the personal and family history, and try and describe the psychic pain of the suicide . . . but most of all I want to understand.

I would be so grateful if you would consider my request. I would be willing to come to Los Angeles to meet with you if that would help to facilitate the psychological autopsy. To be quite frank, I'm not sure I understand all that would be required. I'm enclosing a section from my work in progress along with a book of my poems. Many of the poems in my first collection refer to my sister's suicide (see *The End of Desire*, pages 20, 21, 32, 70).

Yours sincerely,

Jill Bialosky

RED IS THE STRANGEST PAIN TO BEAR

There were periods during which I could allow myself to think of Kim and other times when it would sink me. Time had formed a seal over the tenderness of my emotions. But from time to time the seal cracked. Mourning the loss of a suicide is a different kind of grieving. It has little to do with the five stages of grief or with any known timetable. Grief is tangled up with complicated feelings of shame and stigma, unsettling feelings about the past, and guilt. Always guilt. It throws into question existential notions about God and the meaning of life itself. When something so terrible can happen, it makes us unsure of how much to trust what we think we know about another person. I became acutely sensitive to the sadness and melancholy I sometimes sensed in others and, at times, overwhelmed by fear and anxiety. I wanted to live productively, to write, to excel in my work as an editor, to find pleasure in the things I loved to do. I sometimes looked at Lucas and marveled at his being—his curiosity, how he woke up ready to greet the day. I had never thought so deeply about the nature of a human being nor possessed such a strong desire to protect and care for another person.

I became a voracious reader of the literature on the act of self-annihilation. Fifty-two of Shakespeare's characters kill themselves, the most prominent of which appear in *Hamlet, Romeo and Juliet, Julius Caesar, Othello,* and *Antony and Cleopatra.* It is possible to read *Hamlet,* for example, as a philosophical meditation on suicide. Hamlet is Christian, and to end his life would be against his religion; if he did, he would not be able to avenge his father's death. He asks: "Whether 'tis nobler in the mind to suffer / The slings and arrows of outrageous fortune, / Or to take arms against a sea of troubles, / And, by opposing, end them." Some scholars and psychologists believe *Romeo and Juliet* to be a study on the impulsivity of teenage suicide: two young people meet when they are both in maladjusted and vulnerable states, hoping to be saved by the other. Before Romeo meets Juliet at the party, he is mourning the loss of his previous lover, Rosaline. Anguished, he hopes to "expire the term of a despised life." At the same time, thirteen-year-old Juliet has been told she is to marry an older man she will meet at the party. Distraught over this, to her surprise she meets Romeo and they kiss passionately. Not knowing if Romeo is married, she says if he is, "my grave is like to be my wedding bed."

Along with reading Shakespeare, I read portions of John Donne's *Biathanatos,* a religious defense of poetry—a difficult and strange piece of work that shows how short a distance we've come in the destigmatization of suicide. It was published posthumously, no doubt because Donne was concerned about publishing a work that defended an act that was then considered a sin and, in Europe, illegal. Donne was said to have experienced suicidal feelings most of his life. In his preface to

Biathanatos he admitted his fascination for the act. "Whensoever any affliction assailes me, mee thinks I have the keyes of my prison in mine owne hand," he wrote.

I read Freud, Erikson, and Jung in my attempt to understand the fragility of the mind. I read chapters in Durkheim's *Suicide: A Study in Sociology,* Plato, and Cesare Pavese's diaries and stories, one of which is called "Suicides." Pavese's diaries examine fifteen years of the Italian poet's life prior to his suicide and document his failure with women, the denigration of his literary works, and the loss of his father when he was six. T. S. Eliot's poetry became a constant. *The Wasteland* — "April is the cruellest month" — was written during a desperate time in Eliot's marriage after he had recovered from a physical and mental breakdown. The poem is about mankind's — and the soul's — struggle for rejuvenation, and in moments when I was low I thought of lines from it:

> What are the roots that clutch, what branches grow
> Out of this stony rubbish? Son of man,
> You cannot say, or guess, for you know only
> A heap of broken images, where the sun beats,
> And the dead tree gives no shelter, the cricket no relief,
> And the dry stone no sound of water.

Some of the most important texts and writings on suicide were stacked up on my floor. *The Savage God* by A. L. Alvarez, *The Bell Jar* by Sylvia Plath, the works of Virginia Woolf, Melville's *Billy Budd* and *Moby-Dick,* both of which can be read as studies of suicide. If you came into my little study (which also functions as our dining room) you might be made nervous by the nature of its contents. I became attuned to the nuances of self-murder in literature, in film, in psychoanalytic research. I read lines from Eliot's *Four Quartets* over and over. "Shall I say it again? In order to arrive there, / To arrive where you are, to get from where you are not, / You must go by a way wherein there is no ecstasy."

When I told David that I was writing about Kim, he looked at me not with misgiving or concern, as I feared he might, but instead with understanding and said that he thought I should. "Why wouldn't you?" he said. And I thought, what have I been so afraid of? Hasn't the worst already happened?

I told myself that if I could compose a narrative of the history of Kim and her suicide, however circular, at least I would be giving her a proper mourning. We live in a culture where it is difficult to mourn publicly, to speak of grief, and to question our connections to the living world and our moral responsibilities to others, even the dead. "In order to arrive at what you do not know / You must go by a way which is the way of ignorance," Eliot writes.

I couldn't stop thinking of those lines from *The Wasteland:*

> April is the cruellest month, breeding
> Lilacs out of the dead land, mixing
> Memory and desire, stirring
> Dull roots with spring rain.

So, against my concerns, I persisted. When we turned on the TV later that night, there was a new reality series on called *Survivor.* I had to laugh.

A week after I wrote to him, Dr. Shneidman called me. For some reason I found myself unprepared, as if I had forgotten that I had written to him or never believed he would write back or try to contact me. His voice appeared out of the void, godlike, and for a few brief moments adrenaline flooded my body and I thought to myself, finally there will be answers. He told me that my essay and Kim's story and my poetry had moved him. "But can you help me figure out what happened?" I asked. "If you come see me we can talk," he replied. He described the reason for the psychological autopsy. "To locate the pain. Suicides are in psychological pain. But I have to caution you. There may not be answers."

After the phone call I pondered the idea of going to Los Angeles, talked about it with David, and then uncertainty and dread intervened and I could not bring myself to make the plans. When I think about what stopped me, fear seems the likely answer, though I suspect it was more complicated than that.

I put aside the project. It was too painful and private. The facts of Kim's life and death recorded on paper—her suicide note, obituary, social security card, the contents of her wallet, her student ID, the medical examiner and police examiner's report, her diaries and papers—I put everything in a drawer. Even though I was putting it aside, I told myself that when the need to see Dr. Shneidman resurfaced, I might go. I held on to the possibility as if it were a salve.

I planted tulips in our garden in the country one November, then forgot about them until they came up from the cold earth to announce their beauty. My having forgotten them did not preclude their existence. The tight nutty bulbs were there all those months buried underground, cultivating their thick roots. Seeing the violet and yellow tulips connected me to Kim. At night I took out my pen and again made notes.

One day while cleaning out my drawers and closets, I came across a pair of her red sweatpants with their Shaker Heights high school logo. I remembered how she used to wear them around the house, how her best friend Mary used to sleep over and they'd roll out their sleeping bags, pillows, and blankets to make a bed on her floor. I remembered the long maxi calico dress she wore for her fourth birthday party. How she sat at the head of the table like a princess with the group of her little friends from the neighborhood around her while my sisters, mother, and I took pictures and served her birthday cake. She was the crown jewel at our table.

> Red is the strangest pain to bear;
> In Spring the leaves on the budding trees;
> In Summer the roses are worse than these,
> More terrible than they are sweet:
> A rose can stab you across the street
> Deeper than any knife:
> And the crimson haunts you everywhere—
> Thin shafts of sunlight, like the ghosts of
> reddened swords have struck our stair
> As if, coming down, you had split your life.

These lines of internalized grief are by the poet Charlotte Mew, who took her own life. She had a childhood marred by the painful death of three younger siblings, and later two of her other siblings drifted into madness and were institutionalized. Her poems express the darkness that seeps into a life marked by loss and captures the bleakness of resignation.

No year has been like this that has just gone by;
  It may be that what Father says is true,
If things are so it does not matter why:
    But everything has burned and not quite through.
    The colors of the world have turned
    To flame, the blue, the gold has burned
In what used to be such a leaden sky.
When you are burned quite through you die.

Along with Kim's sweatpants, I came across the spiral notebook with a teddy bear on the cover she used for a journal in high school. My mother gave it to me a few years after Kim died, when she was finally able to go through the private things she had stored in boxes in the basement. Next she gave me the contents of Kim's wallet and her diaries and papers as if unconsciously passing the torch and appointing me keeper of the tomb. True to form, I did not let her down. I read the journal for the first time in the damp, cool basement of the house in Cleveland where my mother still kept Kim's wooden cradle. I was overcome by the private, inner world I discovered hidden there.

Kim wrote in her high school journal:

I need out. Why doesn't my chest stop hurting? I don't think I have any tears left to cry. I wish I would get cancer or something so I could just die. I don't want to live anymore this way. It's too unsatisfying. All I am is unhappy, unsure, depressed. I need a way out. Please help!

In my own apartment years later, reading her words, with her looped handwriting and her doodles in the margins, the energy and conviction necessary to continue to probe Kim's life and death returned and it was as if I was an archaeologist uncovering the relics of the past, searching for truth from fragments.

TWO LIVES

I am at the beach with my son for three weeks in August—David is with us on the weekends—and during the day while Lucas is at camp I attempt to reconstruct Kim's teenage years. The prevailing belief of suicide is that not everyone who is melancholy or in mental distress is suicidal, and so it is the internal, furtive, invisible world I know I need to uncover to understand her inner turmoil and to re-create the sketchy map that led to her last days.

Lucas never knew Kim, though he has seen pictures of her in our home and in the photograph albums he loves to look at of my family and me when I was a child. For years I couldn't bring myself to tell him that Kim had committed suicide. The word "committed," so firm and unequivocal—how did it come to be a euphemism for the act of suicide? *Webster's* defines "commit" as "to put into charge or trust; consign."

To consign oneself to death.

And yet I wonder how consigned can a twenty-one-year-old ever be to dying?

"She died in a car," I told Lucas when he was four or five, not wanting to lie to him. I suppose I was protective of him. I did not yet want suicide to enter into his worldview or consciousness. And once I told him that my sister had ended her life, how would his view of his mother, and the family I had grown up in, change? Would I explain to him that people live not through one lifetime but through many unconscious layers of suffering passed down, a legacy more formidable than anything he'd ever imagined? In the first picture Lucas saw of Kim, she was about the age he was then, seven or eight, perched on her small bicycle, wearing a Cleveland Indians T-shirt. Every now and then he'd bring it up again. "How did she die again, Mom?" he'd ask, wanting more details, intuiting that I was holding back. There was something about the way she looked in her photographs that enchanted him, her warm eyes squinting as she smiled. "It makes me sad to talk about," I told him. Sometimes he pushed for more details and I grew uncomfortable. Finally, when he was in the sixth grade, I sat at the foot of his twin bed and knew I could not lie to him anymore. I said that Kim had been very sad and that she had taken her life. "Now and again life gets too painful and a person can't see out of it, can't let anyone inside, and that's what happened to Kim," I explained, surprised by how simple it sounded.

My mother, a product of the fifties who left college after a semester to marry and begin a family at the age of twenty, survived by doing whatever she needed to get through each day. In our house, like most of that era, there was no language to explain loss, death, separation, and disharmony. Like so many of her generation, she lived an unexamined life. Is there a connection between an unexamined life and the pull of self-annihilation? The delirium of unknowing or refusal to know encases the individual in a detached universe not unlike the suicide's disengagement from the world of the living. But perhaps remaining unconscious, to a certain extent, is simply a coping mechanism for dealing with emotional anguish. Of the failure to examine our inner self, the poet Lucille Clifton, in her poem "the light that came to lucille clifton," writes: "she could see the peril of an / unexamined life / she closed her eyes, afraid to look for her / authenticity / but the light insists on itself in the world."

Even as I write this, I understand how easily things can be missed. Lucas is now thirteen. I worry about him suddenly shutting down and not speaking to me. Even the most caring and conscious parent, caught up in his or her own concerns, can make mistakes and miss things.

Lucas persists in wanting to know more details about the suicide. Now that he's thirteen, I can no longer dodge it. I also make him promise to tell me when there's something bothering him, or if he's in trouble. I tell him how important it is not to keep secrets. "I know why, Mom," he says. "It's because of Kim."

When a person is suffering from despair, anxiety, unease, or depression, there is often no physical manifestation that lets others know she is hurt. As far as I knew, Kim did not have the symptoms often associated with depression such as loss of appetite, energy, and sociability. As a teenager, her inner fragil-

ity and insecurities were already masked, as they so often are.
In fact, I wonder if it is those who don't talk about their pain
who are at greater risk? During the teenage years young people
begin to process the events and experiences of childhood and
form their own identities. Perhaps, along with physiological
reasons, that is why teenagers need more sleep, as though the
unconscious is working overtime to catch up. It is the time, if
a teenager is secure, when he or she can risk enough to try to
separate from his or her parents. I want to study these years
and pinpoint the exact moment when everything went awry.
This desire is partly delusional. I know this. Still I persist. It
is part of my process of forgiving myself. I want to reassure
myself that even had I been aware of all Kim's vulnerabilities, I
wouldn't have suspected she was suicidal.

I work for a few hours and then I pick up Lucas from camp. A
trapeze is on the front lawn. Under the tent children are talking to one another, throwing water balloons, laughing. When
I'm with a group of children I often watch them closely. My
eye sometimes seeks out the child who looks sad and troubled.
I'm aware of the fragility inside every child. When a friend or
colleague confides an emotional problem with her child, I can
catch myself becoming overly involved, too intense. I know
the worst can happen. I watch mothers dressed in their tennis
whites or their bikini cover-ups just off the beach drive up in
their cars to fetch their children. They seem without worry, un-
burdened, different from me. I think that, instead of being an
observer, I should join in. But really what I think is that if Kim
hadn't ended her life, I would be different—more carefree, less
worried, more like the other mothers I see.

Lucas gets in the car. He's hot. He's been playing outside all day. He's irritable. After a solitary morning of writing, I want him to go to the beach with me, but I know that all he wants to do now is go home, have a cold drink, and play a video game in his air-conditioned bedroom. I take him back home, and while he's unwinding in his bedroom I go out to the pool and have a swim.

When I swim my mind is focused on putting one arm in front of the other and the feel of the cool water. Sometimes, in that half-present, half-unconscious state, things percolating under the surface emerge. As I struggle to figure out what happened to Kim, I am alive and engaged and purposeful. But writing about my mother's periods of depression and Kim's insecurity as she moved into adolescence results in periods of psychic unrest and visceral unease. If I think too carefully about what I am doing, I turn a critical eye on myself. Just as I want to be more like the apparently carefree mothers at the camp pickup, I wish momentarily I could be another kind of writer— clever, funny—even though I know self-recrimination is part of the writing process and that writers don't always choose what they need to write about. "I couldn't bear to have my book (my life) wait hidden inside me like a dead child," the poet Robert Lowell said in a letter to Elizabeth Bishop in describing the personal poems he wrote about the breakup of his marriage, poems that were criticized for liberties he took appropriating phrases from his wife's letters to him within his verse.

How would Kim feel about having her private life probed and reinvented through my words? Am I doing justice and honor to her experience? Would she be pleased? On this too-sunny day I am seized by serious moral questions and uncertainties, trying to determine what is permissible. Is my own discomfort about suicide threatening to thwart my efforts to tell her story? Is the desire to push painful memories away a necessary part of survival, or what ultimately hinders recovery? Am I able to make her story universal? Avoid self-pity and blame? I tell myself that, if I can portray her inner world, it may offer a window for other readers to understand the fragility of the suicidal mind. But am I just deluding myself?

A mind considers an event, takes it in, distances itself, and filters it through its own subjective lens. Nothing is fixed, and no single perspective is more truthful or meaningful than any other. Perhaps by now, after so many years have passed, I can only mythologize Kim, as we do once time has put some distance between the past and the present. Isn't it true that even in writing memoir, individuals portrayed become characters? Perhaps I can only see Kim through the lens in which I'd like to view her. Or does shame make certain truths impossible to face? Emily Dickinson wrote of shame:

> Shame is the shawl of Pink
> In which we wrap the Soul
> To keep it from infesting Eyes —
> The elemental Veil
> Which helpless Nature drops
> When pushed upon a scene
> Repugnant to her probity —
> Shame is the tint divine.

The great tragedy is that knowledge — even incomplete — comes late. I can never bring Kim back. And yet, irrationally, through writing, a part of me believes I can. In *The Year of Magical Thinking*, Joan Didion writes about the sudden shock of her husband's death and the year in which she could not face that he was gone. Keeping his shoes in the closet meant he might come back. In mourning a suicide, disbelief persists and with it the magical thinking that one can still reverse the past to change the course of what happened.

The Aristotelian notion of tragedy is defined as a drama that depicts the suffering of a heroic character who "is often overcome by the very obstacles he is struggling to remove." Shakespeare, (here I think of Hamlet or King Lear) recognizes the significance of personal and communal history on an individual. Aristotle posits that when the audience experiences the tragedy, they are able to rid themselves of their own emotions the drama evokes, as they, as witness, become part of the drama. I'm aware that inherent in my writing of Kim's suicide is my desire to rid myself of my own suffering by acting out the drama. If I can make sense of the incomprehensible, then I am redeeming Kim and in memory she remains unscathed. But am I doing it for her or me?

When I step out of the pool, dry off, and go back into the house, Lucas is in the kitchen, biting into a fresh peach. "I'm ready to go the beach now, Mom," he says, planting a kiss on my cheek, as if all along he's known what I needed. "Come on, get your stuff. Let's go."

part four

TEENAGER

I like to keep her here: young and alive and about to experience the wonders of first love, so many years away from the horror of the night when she left us. I have only to close my eyes to picture her. Once the braces were off, and her body had grown long and lean, she ventured outside the protective walls of our family. She hung out in a pack, with her trio of best friends. Sometimes I'd come home and they'd be shut inside her room, lying on her carpet or sprawled on the beds, smoking cigarettes, laughing, trying on clothes or putting on makeup, plotting a rendezvous.

They went to Mentor-on-the-Lake, their string bikinis showing off their astonishingly beautiful bodies, listened to disco or rock on the boom box, looked out for boys. They slept over at each others' houses, went to the movies, cruised in their cars, stayed up late talking on the phone. Before they went to bed they studied their pimples in the mirror, rubbed a white mask of Noxzema on their skin. It would have been hard to predict, long hair streaming down their backs as they gossiped and laughed, which one of the four would not make it.

When I looked into Kim's eyes in those days, they were like mirrors calling me back to my adolescent self. I watched her sit near the phone in her bedroom, which had once been mine. She was fifteen, smitten with her first boyfriend. *It's so nice to be happy,* she wrote in her journal. After they'd had a fight, she would come down to the breakfast table wearing sweatpants and a baggy T-shirt, eyes swollen. Boys, with their sexual magnetism, sweaty brows and hands, and crafty ways of making their interests known, had taken priority in her life.

She was infatuated to distraction, as so many girls are, with her first boyfriend. He was tall and lanky with longish cork-screw curls and a dimpled smile. She shrieked with delight at the playful way in which he made her laugh or teased her, and looked at him with a worshipful look in her eyes. Like any girl on the precipice of adulthood, she stepped shyly from her circle of friends and family, as if from a warm bath, into his cocky, boyish arms.

Once Kim and her best friend came to visit me in New York. I took them to an Irish pub on 79th Street (a pub I still pass often and haven't entered since, afraid of the memories) and felt that wild sense of recklessness from my own youth inside the smoky room as the beer-intoxicated college-age guys checked out Kim and her friend as they sidled through the crowd.

Kim's black and white cat Gretel would only sleep in her room. He knew her gentle goodness. Everyone did. The needy were attracted to Kim like metal to a magnet. Kim loved our two old-fashioned great aunts, daughters of immigrants: Aunt Harriet, who used to bake cookies with Kim on Saturdays, and Aunt Florence, who never married and lived by herself in an apartment in Shaker Square, reading romance novels at night, afraid of her own shadow. Both aunts dressed for every occasion in their matching sweater sets and wool skirts.

Aunt Harriet and Aunt Florence fussed over Kim, the way they did over us older sisters and over my mother when she was a child. Aunt Florence used to call Kim and ask her if she was wearing a sweater because she was afraid the house was drafty and she'd catch a cold. If Kim said no, Aunt Florence told her she would hold on while Kim went to get a sweater. Before Kim had a car, she took the rapid transit to Shaker Square to visit Aunt Florence, who in her seventies still slept in a twin bed with four maple posts, bringing her cookies from our city's famous Hough Bakery where I used to work after school, or bagels from Sand's Deli. Sometimes she'd stay for only ten or fifteen minutes because Aunt Florence worried it was getting dark. And when Kim left, even in the summer, Aunt Florence usually gave her one of the sweaters she used to buy for us girls on sale at May Company downtown and hoard in her closet, still with the tags on.

Kim liked to do things for other people. On one of her report cards from school her art teacher wrote, "Kim is a good citizen." Her seventh-grade math teacher commented, "Kim represents quiet success. She is an excellent student." She was a candy striper. Once she volunteered at a nursing home. She collected door to door for UNICEF. She was the kind of person who always befriended the underdog, the slow boy who lived down the street and mowed our lawn (he was the one who found her dead in our garage), or her best friend when she was little, our neighbor Josh, who was ostracized at school because he was different, the boy whose own sister killed herself when she was a teenager—so many lives the murder of the self has touched.

She also had a playful streak. Here is a poem she wrote for Halloween when she was young.

> *The witches fly*
> *Across the sky*
> *The owls go who? Who? Who?*
> *And the black cats yowl,*
> *And the green ghosts howl*
> *Scary Halloween Boo!*

FIRST LOVE

When Kim was sixteen she'd sit in the living room with her boyfriend and he'd put his arm around her on the couch. Look at that double chin, he'd tease, when she put her head down, and then he'd take his finger and run it up her face from her chin to her nose. "Stop," she'd say, playfully punching him in the arm. He winked at her. He squeezed her knee until she screamed for him to stop. He possessed that proud swagger in his walk that came from knowing his girlfriend adored him. Around him, dressed in her tight T-shirt and cutoff jean shorts that revealed her long, curvy legs, Kim was alluring and fun-loving, too. I understood. When I was her age I was attracted to boys just like him—the kind that liked to play sports, fish, go hiking, drive cars. We were girls who liked to watch others and bask in their radiance. While she was supposed to be writing an essay or working on computation, Kim's mind might have drifted back to the dimple in his cheek when he smiled. And when he didn't call her for a few days because he didn't want her to get too close, or because the intensity of her beauty may have gotten under his skin and made him feel weak, she worried he no longer loved her. Her longings were deep and unmanageable. *Why can't I be smart and beautiful and lovable? Why did his feelings change? What did I do that made him love me less?* she wrote in her journal.

She became too attached too quickly, as if the collision of emotions that love unleashed had opened vulnerable channels inside her. She was confused by her own complicated emotions. Kim wrote in her journal about her fears of being abandoned. I began to ponder the journal more closely after I'd digested the police and autopsy reports, hoping to understand her state of mind. I was upset to learn from her journal that she may have thought of suicide during this period in her life when, beginning her first relationship, she ought to have been happy. In an entry dated 11/4/85, five years before her death, she wrote: *I really wish I didn't have to put up with my life. Sometimes I get a funny feeling in my chest. . . . It's sort of like something is the matter and I can't grasp what.* On another page she wrote, *I wish I could get cancer or something so I could just die.*

On a different page she created a chart. One heading she titled "Fears" and underneath it she wrote, "car accident, being alone, insecurity." Another column she titled "What Was Once Loved But Not Now" and underneath, "popularity, being with family," and in the middle the word "suicide." Though the meaning of this part of the chart is more difficult to decipher, I believe she held out suicide as an option if her fears and pain proved too great. At sixteen or seventeen, she did not yet possess the self-knowledge to connect the engulfing need and anxiety she experienced each evening after her boyfriend left, wondering if he'd return, with the insecurities that had manifested in her after her father left her. Instead Kim blamed herself for the scope of her inner unrest. Given her father's abandonment of her, is it any wonder she focused so much energy on avoiding another painful separation? In a book about daughters and absent fathers called *Father Loss,* I read that many daughters who have been abandoned by their fathers—through death, separation, or abandonment—will try to hold on to an intimate relationship, even when it isn't satisfying.

Most revealing were Kim's words at the end of the chart where under the heading "A Want" she listed, "confidence, a love, independence." Under "What Would You Give for a Person You Love" she wrote, "loyalty, my life, myself."

FEAR	WHAT WAS ONCE LOVED BUT NOT NOW	A WANT	WHAT WOULD YOU GIVE FOR A PERSON YOU LOVE
car accident	popularity	confidence	loyalty
being alone	suicide	a love	my life
insecurity	being with family	independence	myself

A PROSE POEM IN TWO VOICES USING EXCERPTS FROM KIM'S DIARY

What do you do when someone is always on your mind?
All I do is think and want, what can I do? I hate it. Oh, girls who are hungry. You sit at the table and watch the kitchen

clock. Tick tock. You paint your toenails, wash your hair, leave behind your pink princess dress, butterfly wings, braided hair. You smoke cigarettes, drink beer, watch your heart in your chest leave you like a wheel rolling down a hill. *If it's going to be without him I need to start now. It's not getting easier. It's getting hard. Please help me. I need some happiness. I hate him for doing this to me. I need to know what happened. I am about the weakest person in the world. I've called him twice. How am I supposed to get through this? Everybody says it's going to take a lot of time. Well, I can't do it. Things happen too fast. Little things can change your whole life in such a small amount of time. Love is a feeling that is supposed to last forever. It's so strange that it should always be there. How can one fall in love so quickly then? It is so confusing. It changes your life.* Oh, to be loved and cherished. *It's so much fun to make him happy, it makes me happier to make him happy. Watching his face light up when I do something nice is the best feeling in the world.* And how certain you become that your love will not be returned. *I've put a lot of myself into this. Probably more than I should have, I wanted to get a lot out of it too. I hope that we are always good friends, even when it is over.* And what little pleasure remains in the journey. *I've realized that I do love him, too much. It hurts so much when the love isn't returned. I can see that he can get along well without me and I can't without him. What should I do? It's scary to see that the feelings are so deep. I don't know how I can change my feelings for him, but I realize that I have to because it will just get deeper and hurt a hell of a lot more.* How you obsess and grieve and connive for your tender hearts. *I made myself very vulnerable last night. I said I missed him,*

*and implied that I wanted and needed him back. He said
he missed me too. Tonight I am supposed to see him for the
first time since we broke up. I'm afraid it will be the last
time. I've got to get together the thing that I'll say. I've got
to plan and make him realize that he misses and needs me.
When he sees that then I will work my hardest to make everything work out. I don't want to cry anymore. I was so
strong the other night when this happened, but now I have
about the strength of my old self. Why can't I be smart and
beautiful and lovable? Why did his feelings change? What
did I do that made him love me less? I think everyone needs
some sense of security. To feel wanted by someone. Mine is
my fucking teddy bear now. I have to hold him when I sleep
or else I'm scared. My plan now is to turn mean. Blow-off
my friends and family and make everyone hate me. If nobody cared then it would be easy to leave. I'm so trapped.
There is no place I could go if I wanted to leave.* And your
fathers? Where o where art thou? *Since the loved one becomes a part of you, you must not lose him. The thought of
loss is frightening.* In the margins of your journals you draw
little hearts.

*Do I love him? Yes I do. More than anything. Then why
are you asking. Because he doesn't love me.*

FATHER

Once, some years earlier, before Kim reunited with her father,
I was back home from college for the summer and working at

one of the finer restaurants in the neighborhood. I was in my early twenties. I went to greet a new party of six who had just been seated in my station and found to my dismay my stepfather seated at the head of my table, surrounded by a group of friends dressed in tennis whites clearly just off the tennis courts. Next to him was the woman he had left my mother for; she was a platinum blonde, buxom and tall. He was the man at any dinner who commanded the attention of the rest of the table. And on that day he was cheerful and imposing, too.

He was the man who once took me with him alone on a trip to Pittsburgh to meet his mother. Who used to sit next to me on our couch while he watched *The Honeymooners*, his favorite show. When Jackie Gleason sent Alice to the moon, our couch shook with his laughter. He was the man I once made a birthday card for out of cutout pictures and phrases from magazines like "perfect golfer" and "best dad ever." This man once shared my mother's bed and knew intimate secrets about my family. I hadn't seen him since he came to pick Kim up when she was thirteen. It seemed impossible that he was at the restaurant where I worked. My first impulse, out of fear and awkwardness, was to turn and walk out the door. I couldn't serve him or his friends. Instead another waiter covered for me while I spent the rest of my shift out back behind the kitchen, bewildered by the strange feeling inside me that more bad was to come. I wish I could say I had had the courage to approach him, say, "Hello, remember me, Dad?"

As I stood outside the restaurant, I wondered how it was possible that Kim's father, who had once lived with us, was now sitting at my table, in my station at the restaurant, with seemingly no real connection to my family anymore, except that biologically he was my sister's father. I wondered, had I approached his table, if he would have recognized me and, if so, how he would have reacted.

When a boy was in her company, Kim lit up her twinkling, innocent smile. Love me, it said, don't hurt me. I know I'm not good enough. Please stay. Some girls never stop craving the love of their fathers. Losing a father, whether through death or divorce, leaves a young girl with feelings of shame. "To have a parent who is missing, is to live in a shadow of something ominous," writes Elyce Wakerman in *Father Loss*.

The impact fathers have in young girls' lives is strange and compelling. Of the shades of its lasting power, I am reminded of Shakespeare's poem from *The Tempest:*

> Full fathom five thy father lies;
> Of his bones are coral made;
> Those are pearls that were his eyes;
> Nothing of him that doth fade,
> But doth suffer a sea-change
> Into something rich and strange.

Shakespeare's phrase "full fathom five" ironically became the title for one of Sylvia Plath's first poems about her mercurial relationship with her father, who died when she was nine. In the poem Plath describes her wish to join him in the deadly sea. Of his commanding power she writes, "You defy questions; You defy other godhood."

Though there were varying shades of sadness, confusion, and disappointment in our house when the marriage between my stepfather and my mother turned bad, it wasn't until recalling the incident at the restaurant that I fully absorbed that his leaving had hurt me, too. Unconsciously, as Kim did—*Dear Father, why won't you be my dad?*—I took it to mean that we were unworthy of being loved.

BEACH

I am at the beach where I sometimes go to walk after a morning of writing. I could watch the waves forever, the way they sprawl out over the sand and then curl inward again. The consistent sound as they slap the beach as if to say, Wake up, don't waste a minute. You only have this one life. The sea gives and takes. Restores a sense of balance. Leaves a taste of salt on the skin. The wind carries the stench of the life beneath the surface and with it the ghosts from the city of the dead. On the beach a feather from a gull, a piece of jellyfish skin, the hard shell of a crustacean, an abandoned tennis shoe. And everywhere white stones and the sting of salt and the sound of her voice calling out to me like the hollow sound inside a shell when it is quiet and I am not afraid to listen.

BABY IN WAITING

I imagine Kim ticking off the days in the calendar, hoping for her period. When it was no longer prudent to deny she was late, she confided in my mother and, after a pregnancy test, discovered she was pregnant. Following Kim's wishes, my mother made arrangements to have the pregnancy terminated. I had gone home to see her. When I entered her bedroom she was lying on her bed, surrounded by pillows and her stuffed animals; one was a big white polar bear. Her hair was tied back in a ponytail save for a few wisps around her forehead. She was dressed in a long T-shirt, holding a pillow against her abdomen, still in pain from the medication she was given to induce cramping in order to shrink her swollen uterus back to size.

"Hi Jilly," she said when I sat down at the foot of her bed. "I'm sorry, honey," I replied, caught in the tug-of-war I often found myself in about whether I should behave like her sister or her mother.

What was in her thoughts, I wondered. It would not have been like her to tell me. It must have seemed unreal: the embryo she had conceived with the boy who slipped into her bed late at night, having crawled through the window, all for naught; the mornings when she must have counted back the days, trying to remember her last period; the ache of her tender breasts and sudden waves of nausea; the beer and food that must have tasted funny. In spite of being conflicted about what to do, she was no doubt filled with that special feeling that she had achieved this one miraculous thing with the boy she loved. Had she been born in another era, lived in a different social milieu, would she have kept that child? And would that have protected her, kept her?

When I read the passages in her journal she kept of the year when love for a boy filled her with joy, and sometimes its flip side, despair, I was surprised to learn how emotionally tied she had become to the baby. I don't know why that surprised me. I think it may have been because in my mind I still thought of her as a young girl and did not want to think that the experience had left a mark. The entry was dated May 8, 1986. She was seventeen. In the diary she wrote: *I wish I had my baby back.* She wanted her baby to hold. She said she wanted to turn her baby into *all the things I'm not but wish I were. I've lost my dreams,* she wrote, as if the baby alone would embody her dreams and hopes.

In reading her words I recalled lines from a Sylvia Plath poem called "Moonrise" about a miscarriage, where the speaker in the poem, riddled with guilt, imagines a fetus not having the chance to be born and herself walking out of the hospital free of attachment:

> White petals, white fantails, ten white fingers.
>
> Enough for fingernails to make half-moons
> Redden in white palms no labor reddens.
> White bruises toward color, else collapses.
>
> Berries redden. A body of whiteness
> Rots, and smells of rot under its headstone
> Though the body walk out in clean linen.

I did not want to imagine how Kim felt when she awoke from the anesthesia, the embryo having been vacuumed from her uterus, the hospital room sterile and cold. My mother was beside her when she woke, no doubt holding out to her a glass of water and giving her a comforting smile.

Later that night, when I checked on Kim in her bedroom, she was curled up in the fetal position facing the white and gold floral wallpaper I had stared at, too, when it had been my room and I was in fear of what I had done—conceived like her a child out of carelessness and a false sense of invincibility—and she used to tumble into my bed. We talked a little and I asked her about her boyfriend and why he hadn't come to see her. She looked disappointed. "Your guess is as good as mine," she said. Her eyes were so unhappy she blinked with the weight of it. "He probably couldn't handle it. How are you?" she asked, to change the subject. "How's New York?"

Instead of answering her questions, I told her about the time I had had an abortion, when I was a few years older than she was then, hoping it might make her feel less alone. She listened, as she always did, but it was hard to read her. She was a girl of few words. She pressed her face against the fur on her polar bear to hide the embarrassment in her eyes. When I asked her how she was, she smiled, the kind of smile you make to hold back tears. "I'm okay," she said, a history of dark tender nights in her voice. She pulled back the covers and suddenly sprang to her feet in a graceful motion like a cat wanting to escape, to go to the bathroom, perhaps to cry.

Sisters are mirrors. We see parts of ourselves in each other. I wonder if she saw in me the reflection of a whole and safe life like a mirage just outside her grasp. I knew she felt that she was disappointing me. When she was going through a rough time and had lost her path, I worried that because we were older, more settled in our lives, she felt separate from the original family of sisters. When she called to wish me a happy birthday three days before she died, and we talked together about my pregnancy, I wondered whether she thought I was going to leave her behind, that the new life growing inside me was filling her space. She had been my baby. I diapered her, took her on long walks in her stroller, sometimes got up in the middle of the night to feed her. I was her second mother. All three of us older sisters were. On the phone that day I heard a voice that was heartsick and bittersweet and tender. I did not know that her very being was already wrapped like a shroud inside a seal of resignation. I only heard how tired she sounded, though it was midday.

TULIPS

Nearly twenty years after Kim's death, reading Sylvia Plath's poem "Tulips," a disguised narrative about her state of mind in the hospital after a suicide attempt, I hear Kim's sighs and resignation. I am struck by the parallels between the speaker's inner world and Kim's.

> The tulips are too excitable, it is winter here.
> Look how white everything is, how quiet, how snowed-in.
> I am learning peacefulness, lying by myself quietly
> as the light lies on these white walls, this bed, these hands.
> I am nobody; I have nothing to do with explosions.
> I have given my name and my day-clothes up to the nurses
> And my history to the anesthetist and my body to surgeons.

In the poem, tulips become the manifestation of the suicidal self. Like the tulips, the speaker in the poem is too "excited" by the world, too vulnerable to its potency. She lies on
the hospital bed apart from the living. The image of the body
"lying by myself quiet / as the light lies on these walls, this bed,
these hands," is almost corpse-like, a body prepared for burial.
She sees herself alone, separated from mankind, a "nobody,"
having already given up her name, her day-clothes, her responsibilities to society.

> Now I have lost myself I am sick of baggage—
> My patent leather overnight case like a black pillbox,
> My husband and child smiling out of the family photo;
> Their smiles catch onto my skin, like smiling hooks.

Her world has become deeply internalized. Even her beloved family, like "smiling hooks," is dangerous because of how
acutely she feels she has failed them. Yet, still she is attached,
unable to escape their expectations. She sets up barriers between
herself and those she loves, as if to protect herself from them,
and them from her, in the process further alienating herself until
her despair becomes all-consuming.

> I didn't want any flowers, I only wanted
> To lie with my hands turned up and be utterly empty.
> How free it is, you have no idea how free—
> The peacefulness is so big it dazes you,
> And it asks nothing, a name tag, a few trinkets.
> It is what the dead close on, finally; I imagine them
> Shutting their mouths on it, like a Communion tablet.

In the poem, peacefulness resides in fantasies of death, where the world no longer makes its demands, where one might be freed of the pain of despair until one feels "utterly empty" and resigned. The speaker idealizes the promise of peacefulness awaiting her on the other side of life, where she believes she will receive Communion.

> The walls, also, seem to be warming themselves.
> The tulips should be behind bars like dangerous animals;
> They are opening like the mouth of some great African cat,
> And I am aware of my heart; it opens and closes
> Its bowl of red blooms out of sheer love of me.
> The water I taste is warm and salt, like the sea,
> And comes from a country far away as health.

No other poem I know expresses the sense of hopelessness, self-hate—the self, like an animal, belongs caged behind bars—and despair of the suicide as profoundly as "Tulips." Hope resides only in the ability of the speaker to free herself from her anguished state. Health is a dream as distant, far away, and unattainable as a foreign country.

FAIRY TALE

After the abortion Kim started leaving the light on in her bedroom and drew hearts and charts in her journal. Slept with her head by the yellow princess phone. Touched her empty abdomen in the half twilight. Perhaps lying in bed in the solitude of night, when our dreams and imaginings awaken, she thought about her father. *Dear Father, why won't you be my dad?* she had written in her journal. For many years she must have imbued him with magical power. As a young girl, he was the person her imagination revolved around like a beam of light. He was the missing father in every fairy tale and story about a daughter who longs to be rescued.

WARNING BELL

The bittersweet aftertaste lingered in the quiver in her smile, the flashes of anger that gave over to sadness when her boyfriend's name came up. Again, the conundrum: how he could be there one minute breathing in her hair, kissing her neck, promising more than he knew in the way he looked at her, and then he was gone, not having said much, just slowly fading away, the way boyfriends did when one is young.

In her high school senior photo she is wearing a magenta sweater. Her hair is combed in place and there is a frosty lipgloss shine to her lips as if she has just fixed herself up in the mirror. She's wearing her wanting-to-please face that belies her inner turmoil. She is the blond girl with the tight jeans, blue cloth binder pressed against her chest, the girl everyone at school flocked around, the girl the boys checked out. Not so good that she wouldn't have a smoke in the girls' bathroom. That kind. But something had changed. It was as if there was a tangle of spiderwebs in her head, distancing herself from herself. Two girls in one.

Perhaps it was the yellow light falling on her desk, the black night through the shuttered blinds, the thinking pulsing numbing drum inside her body, missing her boyfriend, mourning for her baby, the lure of cigarettes and drugs, the confusion of friends and the mirror of achievement they held up too high that distracted her. Looking back, I think it was dread, the feeling that builds those hours after sunset on Sunday night, when the anxiety and fears of the responsibilities of school returned to her—those hours when the world suddenly seems wrapped in a gray blanket.

She fell behind during her last year of high school. Up until then her grades had been strong; suddenly her papers were left unfinished, tests incomplete, and long-term projects not begun. *I'll never finish, be good or smart enough*, she wrote in her journal. I imagine on the days she showed up to school, it was easier to smoke a cigarette in Hippie Hall and hang out with friends than to follow the thread of thought in the classroom; having missed so much, she struggled to keep up. She might have looked around at her many friends who managed to stay on course and wished she could be like them. *It's so nice to be happy.* If there is a particular time that defined the clear yet inaudible sound of a life beginning to unwind, this was it, the moment before her life began to spin off course, like the point in a novel at which everything that has come before turns and past events reveal their significance. Yet we didn't see it.

In my reading about teenage suicide, I learned that there is a program at Columbia University developed by David Shaffer and his colleagues for screening depression and suicidal tendencies in high school students for known predictors of suicide. Surely this program, or a similar program, should be implemented in every high school, given the rate of suicides among teens, because that is when signs of depression or suicidal proclivities often begin to manifest.

Who knew what they did, she and her new best friend, the go-to girl when she needed someone to cut school with? Perhaps they lingered in someone's father's car and passed a joint. Looked out the smudged windows at the gray sky without even a patch of sun to energize the view. Algebra did not make sense. Shakespeare was a foreign language. Besides, there was that rush when she knew what she was doing was bad. It made her feel sort of good. Or maybe she wanted someone to notice her?

The guidance counselor arranged a meeting with her mother and father at school after she'd been caught cutting classes. This might have been the first time the three of them, Kim and our mother and her father, were in the same room together for an extended time since she was three years old. Her father was ticked. Perhaps he had been called out from a business meeting, dressed in his gray suit. "Hi Dad," I imagine she said, looking up at him sitting across from her in the sterile room with walls made of brick, a spark in her eye, happy that he cared enough to come. She didn't see him much. Maybe a few times a year. But quickly she read the disappointment in his look. "I'm sorry," she probably said, looking down at her hands folded tensely in her lap. She told me later, with tears in her eyes, how he had said, "You'll never amount to anything," before he got up and walked down the hall without her, shaking his head, the squeak of his leather shoes resounding on the polished linoleum floor.

It is impossible not to wonder whether the right word or gesture that day might have changed the course. I wish that, sitting in the guidance counselor's office, her father, instead of being hurtful, might have had the insight to know that something else was going on to make her suddenly fall behind. I wish it had occurred to him that he shouldn't have left her all those years, and that he'd make it up to her and help her forge a plan, that her falling behind was a wake-up call. Maybe he might have reached out to my mother, even though she was still bitter about having been left, about being a single parent who wanted and required help raising her daughter. Together they might have put Kim's needs first.

Perhaps if Kim had broken down, all three adults sitting in the stuffy guidance counselor's office, speechless, heads low, would have known what they had to do. Give her back what had been taken from her: a sense of self-worth, tranquillity, a belief that she came first. Things might have turned out differently. Clearly someone should have known that a teenager who has always been a good student, resourceful and bright, who suddenly can't concentrate or complete assignments, who seems not to care, must be burdened by emotional and psychological problems. But instead, like vulnerable, sensitive girls often do, Kim stuffed down her tears, flicked back her hair, and pretended she didn't care.

Not long after that meeting, in what would turn out to be a defining moment, she took up with Alan. He worked behind the counter at the deli and I imagine flirted with her when he made her a turkey sandwich or a toasted bagel. Perhaps he drove by in his beat-up car that smelled of cigarette smoke and pot and a hint of Old Spice, the kind of cologne her father might have worn. "Come on, I'll give you a ride," he might have said. When she got in the car, perhaps he popped in a Bruce Springsteen tape, lit up a Marlboro Light, and looked into her made-up eyes. In the reflection of her side mirror she might have checked the school of tiny pimples partially concealed by Cover Girl makeup on her chin. "Do you want to go out sometime?" he may have said before she scribbled her phone number on the inside leaf of a matchbook. It was around this time that she wrote in her journal:

> *Dear Father—*
>
> *Why won't you be my dad? I'm not perfect, I know that. I'm not even close. But still, I can't be that bad. Maybe I don't live up to your expectations. I tried though. I tried damn hard to, when I realized I couldn't I just gave up. I idolized you. I wanted you to love me as much as I loved you. That's all I wanted. Just love me for me. You could never do that. You never will. I would have done anything for you once, now I can't even afford to get close to you because you'll only hurt me again. Tell me how bad I am and what I do is wrong. . . . It's too hard to have your love only once in a while. Maybe you'll realize one day that I am a good person. Maybe a little screwed up but I'm me and that's good enough for most people. I wish you were like most people.*

It might have been a week or two after the meeting at school—when her father still hadn't called to see how she was doing or offer help, when her mother was ensconced in financial and personal worries—that she made a plan, decided to leave behind the blur of little blue books with smiling faces in the margins and red check marks on the page, and dropped out of school only a semester short. "Are you sure you're doing the right thing?" I asked, worried, knowing that when I was her age being successful at school was my hope of finding a way out.

"I know what I'm doing," she said. "I have a plan." The brochures and booklets to study for the GED were on her bed. "It's not like I'm going to Harvard," she said. She had the ability, with her quick wit, to put on a good face and make you believe in her. In spite of the unease her decision left us with, what else could we do but trust her? Looking back now, I think that by quitting school she was seeking a quick fix to move past her sense of failure.

One thing I know for sure is that I'm scared. I hate school and can't wait to get out. If I'm not going to pass then what's the sense in going? These sentences in her journal I discovered too late. It wasn't until her friends were preparing for the prom in their party dresses and pumps and for graduation in their long black robes and tassel hats that the repercussions of her decision left their humiliating mark: *I have a lot of trouble getting through a lot of things. . . . I feel so empty lately. I wish I were graduating with my friends. I wish I had my baby. I would love to have someone to love and to have someone depend on me. I want my baby! I could teach it and love it and turn it into all the things I'm not but wish I were.*

Perhaps it was after long days of emptiness, when her friends were still in class, the hours lying awake in bed filled with doubts, that she decided to go out with Alan. There was something about him, rough around the edges, with coarse workmanlike hands and a proud strut she liked, as if he contained the darkness and unquenchable rage she sensed in herself, the vortex that she felt would suck her inside if she wasn't careful. It didn't matter that he worked behind the fish counter at the deli where we went to pick up bagels and cream cheese, a carton of milk. She was young. I think he must have courted her for months. Perhaps when he leaned over the counter and winked at her that day she began to see that he was actually kind of sweet. Someone she could talk to, someone to distract her, someone who would hold her and tell her she was beautiful, a knockout, no matter that he was ten years older, a high school dropout and, as she'd discovered later, after she was enchanted, a drug dealer with a criminal record—someone who would lead her down the road to feeling good, blinding her with boyish charisma, then later with vodka tonics, beer, and drugs.

FISH

We have taken the fish in its bowl from the windowsill in our kitchen in the city and brought it with us to the country while we are here for the month of August. Now the bowl sits on a sill that overlooks green flowering trees instead of the red brick of a neighboring building. I go to make a cup of tea and my eye goes to the fishbowl. There is something about watching fish that is soothing and trance-inducing. This is confirmed when we go to check out an assisted-living facility for my mother in Cleveland where there is a fish tank in the main room. We are told that watching fish calms the residents. Our fish is elusive. I look for a second and can't find it. It is resting in the blue marbles, which are the same color as the fish at the bottom of the clear bowl. This fish is slower than the others we've had. Sleepy all the time. Why does this fish sleep so often? I wonder. Or is staying still just another way of being? I have to flick my finger against the glass bowl to make sure it is alive.

FORBIDDEN LOVE

After Kim quit school, she passed the GED exam and worked as a waitress. The tips she collected went to car payments, spike-toed boots, designer jeans, strawberry lipstick, mascara, and eventually college tuition. By this time I was living in New York, had finished graduate school, had begun to publish some of my poems, and had my first toehold in a job in publishing. I wanted the same for Kim and believed she would eventually find her passion, too. I was proud that she'd passed the GED. Many people told me that the exam was more challenging than high school. I was glad she was waitressing and saving money. I told myself she had made a detour but was back on track.

She sometimes hung out at the Beachwood Mall searching for a new outfit, going through the racks at Victoria's Secret or the Gap with one of her friends who had not gone away to college. Sometimes they sprang for happy hour and, as she sipped her margarita, lit a cigarette, laughed with her girlfriends, she might have thought, right here, this moment, this is happiness. But I knew there were stretches of time in the suburbs, especially during a long brutal winter, when she must have become restless, as though she were on a station platform watching the train pass by that would have taken her away. Sometimes she bought pocket-size books of crossword puzzles to pass the time and finished the whole book in one sitting. Or painted her nails. She read popular novels like Rosamunde Pilcher's *The Shell Seekers* as well as literary fiction. She loved Mary Gaitskill's *Bad Behavior* and *Housekeeping* by Marilynne Robinson. I had given her those two books one year for Christmas. Plath's *The Bell Jar* was one of the thirty or so books on the bookcase in her bedroom at the time of her death. It was my own copy, which she must have pilfered from the basement where I stored many of my books from college. Her moods—I can, I can't—swung like a pendulum. In her diary dated 3/27/85 she wrote: *So much of my future depends on what I do now. I've got to get straightened out and start making more out of my life.*

She was thoughtful and sympathetic, belonging more to the world of silences, connecting to the sensitive underside of people, and yet she was never self-absorbed or gloomy or blamed others for her unhappiness. She liked listening to Cat Stevens in her bedroom, and in her journal she copied the lyrics to "Morning Has Broken" next to one of her poems with words and phrases scratched out.

Sometimes I would ring home from my office in New York to check up on her. It would be noon and, while most people I knew were working in offices in towering buildings, typing, answering phones, she'd still be in bed. My mother, perhaps groggy from a sleeping pill or suffering from a migraine, might be, too. It's okay, I told myself, this will pass. During one of our phone calls, when I asked what she was up to, Kim said she was looking into being a stewardess and had gone through the trouble of answering an ad from one of the airlines in the *Cleveland Plain Dealer* and had attended a seminar to learn about how to apply. But a few days later she changed her mind. Another time she said she wanted to be a veterinarian. She loved animals, especially cats. They spoke the same intuitive language. I pleaded with her to move to New York and make a fresh start. But her ambitions took a backseat the more involved she became with Alan.

"Come on, babe," he said, squeezing her shoulder, leading her out our front door and then slipping his hand into the back pocket of her jeans, as if he owned her. How quickly he swept her away from us.

Forbidden love, like that of Juliet to her Romeo, ignites a charged power. Whatever occurs between lovers—the secret meetings, the whispered conversations, the clandestine unions—seems larger and more important than the rest of the world when they are together. Without each other, they tell themselves, they will die. That often is the root of the power of a pact between young lovers. As Shakespeare wrote:

> Now old desire doth in his death-bed lie
> And young affection gapes to be his heir;
> That fair for which love groan'd for and would die,
> With tender Juliet [match'd] is now not fair.
> Now Romeo is belov'd and loves again,
> Alike bewitched by the charm of looks;

But to his foe suppos'd he must complain,
And she steal love's sweet bait from fearful hooks.
Being held a foe, he may not have access
To breathe such vows as lovers use to swear,
And she as much in love, her means much less
To meet her new-beloved any where.
But passion lends them power, time means, to meet,
Temp'ring extremeties with extreme sweet.

The fact that no one whom Kim knew approved of Alan—not her family or her friends—the fact that in her mind it was something forbidden, gave a bolt of necessity to the bond. He was an outsider, like her dad. His sleepy half-closed eyes and loose mouth evoked pity and compassion at the same time.

I imagine he passed her a joint when they drove in his car, taught her his particular way of keeping the smoke in her lungs till it burned before slowly blowing it out. I imagine she liked the feeling, dreamy and nice, as if the world had suddenly become a safe planet to live on. They drove around the city, along roads they knew like the backs of their hands, getting high. Then later to visit his hangout, an after-hours bar called the No Name in a strip mall in University Heights where one of his buddies worked and where he sometimes tended bar. He set up shots of tequila. Showed her how to lick her hand, sprinkle salt on it, then squeeze lime on it, before tossing it back. He was broad, a little beefy, liked to have a good time. And for those few hours when she was just a little high, when he reached over and for a minute pulled her close, it was good enough. I wanted to believe that he was good at heart, at least good enough for Kim to hang her hopes on. I'm sure Kim was the first girl he could trust. Kim told me his mother was unstable, lived in an apartment full of cats. Kim said his father had died when he was a child. It was part of his dark romance. I reimagined Kim's relationship in a poem I wrote called "Ruined Secret" long before she died. Even then, not wanting to, I saw through him. But when he gave her a playful tap on her butt or held her hand and she lit up, my heart was stopped by the beauty and danger of it all.

Ruined Secret

My sister fell in love
with an ex-con when she was seventeen
and swore me to secrecy.
I knew what she loved about him
the night she took me
to his run-down three-family
on the dark side of a Cleveland
I'd never seen before.
On the top floor his mother lived
alone with twenty-some cats
she called Sam.
From downstairs we could hear her
call the cats for dinner
and the sound of their twenty-some
pairs of feet fill her kitchen.
When he heard his mother's voice
through the floorboards
he looked ashamed and lit
one of his non-filter cigarettes
and told us the story of his brother
who was a captain in the Navy.

The smell of danger and lust
was everywhere—

In the sheets crumpled on his bed,
in the small bathroom
wallpapered with rock stars,
the dirt underneath his nails;
his slow-tongued English of the streets.
At night my sister
talked to him on our princess phone
in the lemon-scented bedroom we shared
in whispers, and sighed at what I knew
were his hopeless declarations.
After six months the situation had changed.
My sister refused his phone calls,
and when a dozen red roses arrived,
she dumped them in the trash out back
before mother had gotten home.
Even though months had gone by
and we stopped saying his name,
his soft darkness lived in our room
like a ruined secret.

One day he waited after school
in his run-down Pontiac
and she came home with her eye
bruised and a pair of garnet earrings
in her ears.

She did not know how to get rid
of what she started.
He went to his priest

to ask for salvation
and later that same day
when I was working
at the bakery counter after school
he took me by the arm,
cried, and begged me to forgive him.
In our bedroom we stared at the phone
waiting for the scary thrill
that pumped through our bodies
after the first ring;
but eventually the calls stopped
and I'd find my sister
staring out the window
turning the scarlet posts
on her ear that caught
the light like a bleeding heart.

Kim thought she'd found her soul mate. He was lovable. Undereducated. Wore the hurt of his childhood, and its vulnerability, on his face. He was a drug dealer who had once been in prison. Maybe she thought she could change him. He never quite looked you in the eye. And because in his heart he didn't feel he deserved her, he cunningly learned how to whittle down her self-esteem to make sure she wasn't going to leave him. He dressed in leather or jean jackets (one of his old jackets he gave to her now lives on a hanger in my closet), blue jeans, and construction or cowboy boots. Let his beard grow every day or two so that when he shaved, his face looked as soft as a baby's. In him she had found someone to take care of, and someone to take care of her. They set up house together in his two-family in Cleveland Heights. He bought her roses on her birthday, took her out to nice dinners and once on a trip to the Caribbean. The island of St. Lucia was the only country stamped in her passport. I keep it with the rest of her things in a little box with shiny fake rhinestones and glitter glued on the top my son made for me at camp. Seeing Kim and Alan together, with their arms wrapped around each other, made you want to believe in them, even though you didn't.

She wore sexy black dresses, sheer black nylons, and high heels when they went out; and he showed the pleasure he took in her company by offering her drinks and drugs. There is beauty in love even when it is not the kind you wish for your little sister. I suppose she found someone who needed her more than she needed him. Someone who would love her back. She listened for the idling motor of his car, sprang up when she heard it, rushed out. In the evenings they went to movies, in the summer drove to the beach at the lake in their matching dime-store black shades, sometimes stayed up partying for days. Who knew why or when it went bad, but before then, the fact that he hung out with bouncers in clubs, rolled his own cigarettes, wore chains on his jeans to hold his keys, must have seemed nearly heroic to a girl filled with such longing. They played house together. Adopted kittens. Her favorite was called Mittens. How she loved her cats. Their meowing, purrs and hisses, their little grunts. The way they licked themselves, the feel of their coarse tongues. She boasted that cats have highly advanced hearing, eyesight, taste, and touch, and how sensitive they were. In Mittens it was like she had her unborn baby back.

I listened to her talk about her kittens, Alan, the life she was building in Cleveland, and for the time it seemed enough.

A year or so after she dropped out of high school she enrolled at Cleveland State. She took a composition class where she was required to keep a journal. This is an entry dated 4/18/88:

> *Today is April 18. It would be Mittens' first birthday if she were still alive. Mittens was a kitten that I got a little under a year ago, and I loved her very much. She was the most beautiful cat I have ever seen. Her markings were absolutely great. Her coat was a kind of tiger striped. Her coloring was gray, beige, and brown. She was gorgeous. The reason I named her Mittens is because of her paws. She was born with two extra toes on each of her feet. It made her look as if she were wearing mittens . . . the extra toes made her real clumsy. She used to trip over her own feet all the time, she wasn't what you would call a graceful cat.*
>
> *I guess that my relationship with my pets is somewhat abnormal. I think of them as my kids. I really love my cats. Mittens was my cat though. She loved me best. She always slept right next to me, under the blankets. She used to sleep in between Alan and me and get mad if he tried to cuddle with me. She was really jealous of him. She really had a personality like a person. She really trusted me, that is probably why I feel guilty about her dying.*
>
> *I took her to the vet when she was eight months old so that she could be spayed. The vet said it was a simple operation and he did it all the time. When I went to pick her up she was dead. It was just so unfair. I just hope she knew how much I loved her. I hope she didn't have to suffer at all.*

After reading the composition, I remembered Kim being carried into bed with her parents when she was a baby and

the domestic tranquillity she must have felt. All of us hope to
re-create what we have lost. Our losses become road maps for
our future. Living with Alan in his house—which she imagined
they'd fix up one day when they had money—was like trying
to reclaim what was stolen from her when her father left her
when she was three years old. Alan gave her a ring with a little
diamond about the size of the eye of needle, what we would
call a starter ring, which she twisted around on her finger. Even
though I didn't trust Alan, I thought to myself that it's not
so bad to feel loved. When I got up the nerve, not wanting to
alienate Kim, I asked her about her own ambitions, concerned
that at eighteen or nineteen she had become more focused on
their relationship than on herself. She reached her hand to her
throat and pulled at the skin on her neck, a habit she had when
she was nervous or troubled. "I don't know," she said. Then
her face lit up. "I guess I'd like to have a baby and get married,"
she said.

*When love is shared it is wonderful. It should last for-
ever.*

*Since the loved one becomes a part of you, you must not
lose him. The thought of loss is frightening.*

I should have told her the story of Persephone. How she
was abducted to the underworld by the prince of darkness,
tempted by his seduction, and how even her mother could not
fully rescue her. I should have told her that no one really saves
us, not even the father of the world, Zeus, dressed in his many
guises. I should have told her that it takes years of hard work
and many falls to get out from under our shadows. I should

have told her that it was her sense of futility—if I'm going to fail, what is the use in making an attempt?—that ate away at her own ambitions. I should have told her that in our hearts we all feel we'll never be good, strong, and brave enough. We'll never add up. I should have told her that I suspected if she made something of herself, was too ambitious, her Romeo, whom she believed she could not live without, who had made a profession of numbing out the world with drink and drugs, would try to find a way to hold her back. But part of me was afraid to confront the truth. The tragedy of suicide is that only in its aftermath does everything that came before suddenly seem important and clear.

VOICE OF RECLAMATION

I imagine Kim climbing out of her boyfriend's bed in the early hours once she began her first quarter at Cleveland State. Maybe he was still asleep, slightly hungover, on those days when the world seemed a place she could still navigate. I imagine her creeping into the bathroom, putting on a T-shirt, a fuzzy blue sweater—she loved the color blue—a pair of tight black jeans, brushing her teeth in the cracked porcelain sink. "I'll call you later," she may have said before she closed the door on the still darkness of the house, slipping into her tiny navy blue car with a red racing stripe across the side and driving downtown for her morning class with the sun just peeking above the horizon. She liked the rush of students, the stillness of the classroom just before the professor entered, the acquisition of knowledge like a foreign world inside each one of her books, waiting to be unlocked. I can imagine her unzipping the pencil holder, taking out her pen, putting her thoughts in motion just before she began to write:

> *It's so nice to be happy. It always gives me a good feeling to see other people happy. Bringing joy to others is the best way to bring joy to yourself. . . .*
>
> *Doing things to improve myself takes time, but others gain from it too. When I do well those that care for me are proud. My decision to go back to school is a perfect example. Every person I know is very happy that I made that decision. Getting the support I'm getting makes everything I do a lot easier. It also helps to know that others have that much faith in me.*

THE THINGS LEFT IN HER CLOSET

1. Four pairs of black faux-leather boots

2. One pair of white cowboy boots with fringe

3. Ten pairs of jeans bearing labels from Calvin Klein, Gap, Jordache, Old Navy, and Lee's 501s

4. Laura Ashley bridesmaid dress with cabbage-rose print she wore as the maid of honor at my wedding

5. Pink running shoes

6. Short black sleeveless dress

7. Black leather miniskirt

8. Worn leather jacket

9. Two jean jackets—one extra large that belonged to Alan

10. Three faux-leather purses

11. Flannel button-down work shirt

12. Blue tight-fitting cashmere sweater dress

13. Pair of black spike-heeled pumps

14. Cleveland Browns jacket

THEY MUST BE ALL OR THEY ARE NOTHING

There were days when I'm sure she dreamed of more but quickly told herself that if she asked for little she would not be disappointed. "Asshole," I heard Kim say, because Alan had let her down again. Maybe he told her he was working when she found out he was out with his friends, or he forgot to pick her up after her shift. "It's just so typical," she said in a huff that did not quite disguise that still-loving glint for him in her eyes.

Maybe it was those moments when instead of pushing through her disappointment, she sat at her desk in class and, unable to focus on the lecture, put her mind on Alan and wondered what he was up to, whether he'd get busted or find someone else. She lost sight of the big picture. What would learning algebra problems or studying Mesopotamia give her? If she couldn't concentrate and put a one-hundred-percent effort into her course work, what was the sense in continuing? Even though she was going back to school, she seemed not to sustain enough optimism to overcome her doubts and stay the course. Though she may have presumed she'd always live in Cleveland, have the same friends, the same boyfriend, the sheen on the portrait of her future had begun to fade slightly.

In reading about teenage suicide, I learned that perfectionism is a common thread among suicidal patients and that the demands of living up to this uncompromising attitude may become a construct for a teenager's sense of failure and hopelessness. Hopelessness can lead to suicidal thoughts and these thoughts can lead to suicidal attempts. *If I can't finish, then what's the sense in trying,* Kim wrote in her journal. It is likely that the standards she set for herself were so impossibly high that she simply gave up trying to meet them. She saw herself as being all or nothing at all. I think of Shakespeare's lines: "My thoughts be bloody / or be nothing worth."

Some young people who take their own lives are the opposite of the stereotypical rebellious youth. They are anxious and insecure, with a desperate desire to be liked and to fit in and do well. Their expectations are so high that they demand too much of themselves and so are bound to be constantly disappointed. Instead, they try to mask these feelings of disappointment by presenting a persona that is not interested in succeeding. When I tried to pin Kim down about her plans for school, she'd reply in two- or three-word answers, arching her neck back or lighting a cigarette: sort of, I don't know, I'll figure it out. She grew more elusive and vague, afraid of disappointing those of us who cared, hiding like the fish in the coral prison of its bowl.

Because she was afraid of being revealed as an impostor, and a burden to everyone, Kim worked scrupulously at disguising her vulnerability. It wasn't hard to do with her pleasing looks. But internally she was filled with punishing self-disdain. Two weeks before the American poet Hart Crane killed himself, filled with self-hate, he slashed to bits with a knife the painting a friend, the Mexican artist David Siqueiros, painted of him, beginning with his eyes.

In trying to understand why Kim floundered and could not find her course, I turned to the psychological literature. Her identity was in what the psychologist Erik Erikson called "embryonic darkness." The teenage years into the early twenties are a period during which we discover who we are or are going to be. Filled with self-doubt, Kim was caught between her family's expectations of her and her own feelings of diminishment. Sometimes dropping out of high school or college, flirting with drugs and sex, may lead a young person to find her own voice. She may be in the middle of a crisis and must go to the other side before finding out what matters to her. Those who weather the storm sometimes emerge as people of talent and creativity; the birth of creativity can come from the risk of intense self-annihilation. And the sensitive, at times self-destructive, tentative person is perhaps someone who lives at the balance of these two conflicting forces.

Sometimes I saw one side of Kim—a flash of the girl with the knowing smile—and then it would vanish. And then I'd see another side—anxious, serious, a dull look, like a dirty penny in her eyes.

SUICIDE WATCH

When I was seventeen, one of my high school friends was a girl I'll call Sara. Sara was going out with another friend, Nick. Sara was very beautiful. She had a long, thin, shapely body, perfect straight blond hair, dimples in her cheeks when she smiled, and a nervous laugh. She could laugh at anything, and sometimes she laughed so hard her laughter would stop a room. Nick and I could talk for hours, we had that kind of connection, and yet both of us were going out with people we had little in common with. Such is the paradox of attraction.

When Sara and Nick fought he would call me and often tell me about the problems he was having with Sara, frustrated sometimes by her ostentation. Although I liked having his confidence, I found myself trapped in a triangle in which I always felt disloyal. Sara sometimes slept at my house to escape her strict Catholic parents, who did not approve of Nick. One night when she was sleeping over I fell asleep while she was talking to Nick on the phone. They were fighting again, and I was bored by the same drama that seemed by then to repeat itself almost nightly, though on this night—I would learn later—Nick was finally finished with their game playing and broke up with her. My mother was out that night on one of her dates, which meant that our house was a free-for-all.

While I was asleep Sara went upstairs to my mother's bathroom, downed the contents of a vial of sleeping pills she found in my mother's medicine cabinet, and then called Nick to tell him what she'd done. Nick banging on the front door awakened me. Sara was sound asleep by then, a sleep so deep she might not have awoken. Nick told me what had happened and we called an ambulance. Once her stomach was pumped and she was admitted into Hanna Pavilion, the psychiatric unit of University Hospitals, Nick and I talked about what Sara had done. We were bewildered and frightened and wondered whether Sara's suicide attempt was a bid for attention. But now I think it was a wake-up call. She had always been a performer, a tap dancer (I used to be envious of the pink patent-leather suitcase that she carried to school in which she kept her tap shoes), and that night she performed her most memorable act. In all the years I knew her, she had never talked about her inner life—though, to be fair, did any of us? After she returned from her stay in the hospital we tiptoed around her, afraid of her newly revealed vulnerability, as if she were a porcelain doll that might break. How long had she been suffering? What lay behind her dimpled cheeks and impenetrable exterior?

It wasn't until Kim ended her life that I remembered that night long ago when the ambulance descended on our house, its red light whirling a sign of warning. Sara was one of my closest friends and yet she never told me she was unhappy or struggling, although she had complained that her parents were too strict and I had gleaned they embarrassed her. She was fun-loving—silly and bubbly and gay—but underneath her superficial persona were layers of unexplored darkness and insecurity. When Sara's panic-stricken parents came to our front door to find out what had happened to their daughter, I felt culpable and ashamed—she'd taken the pills from my mother's medicine cabinet, under my watch. Not once, in all the following years, even after we'd reconnected at a high school reunion—Sara now married, a mother, and successfully employed—did we ever revisit that night when, save for a stroke of luck, she might not have had a future.

A few years ago, I learned that one of Sara's younger brothers was found dead in his car after having driven into a tree. Accident or suicide? Are we always the masters of our own complicated lives?

Thirty thousand Americans kill themselves every year, and nearly half a million make a suicide attempt medically serious enough to require emergency-room treatment. Psychiatrist Andrew Slaby asserts that "Suicide attempts are really failed suicides." A suicide attempt remains the single best predictor of suicide and, of course, must never be ignored as simply attention-seeking behavior. After an attempt, or even when no attempt has been made but someone is suicidal, he or she should be watched twenty-four hours a day until it is certain the suicidal impulse has passed. If he or she is lucky enough to get into treatment, the strategy is to buy time in which the therapist can begin to access his or her inner world and create a relationship of trust. Each day that a suicide attempt is forestalled brings the suicidal person closer to possible recovery. Because the suicidal person, described by some as a ticking time bomb, resides in a delicate state, one event, like a breakup with a boyfriend, a humiliating event at school, or even a DWI, can function as the catalyst for a suicide.

According to statistics, about a third of people who attempt suicide will repeat the attempt within one year and about 10 percent of those who threaten or attempt suicide eventually succeed in carrying out the act. It is remarkable how many failed suicides precede an actual suicide.

Tapping out these pages on my white MacBook, in the half-lit dining room of my apartment, it is strange now to see the three of us in my mind's eye: Nick and Sara and my younger self, still alive and talking and passionate, as if all that existed in the world was the three of us.

Why was Sara discovered and not Kim? How did Nick know that night to take her words seriously? What if he hadn't? Luck. Fate. Miracle. "The ungraspable phantoms of life." I think of Sara falling asleep on the twin bed across from me like Sleeping Beauty so many years ago, waiting for her prince to wake her with a kiss. The night of Sara's attempt, my sister Kim, just a young girl of seven, was tucked under her calico blanket, asleep in her bedroom upstairs.

GENETIC LINK TO SUICIDE

When my friends talked to me about Kim and her suicide, some inferred, knowing about my mother's history with depression, that there was a genetic component to it. Mental illness, depression, and suicide have afflicted my family. My great aunt Florence's twin sister suffered a breakdown when she was eighteen and was institutionalized. Only recently, when I accompanied my mother to see a new physician and she was giving her family history, I learned that her maternal grandfather had ended his own life. A few years ago, my mother's first cousin committed suicide. Counting Kim's suicide, that makes three suicides in three generations of one family.

When I thought further about families and mental illness and depression—which some psychologists have described as anger turned against the self—I wondered what family has not at one time or another been touched or marooned by these afflictions. What person has not suffered periods of anxiety, sleeplessness, intense doubt, and terror over his or her life choices, over what could have been and may not? And how many families have suicide as part of their history or hidden history? I read that, statistically, once a suicide happens within a family, it increases the risk of suicide for other family members. One 2003 Swedish study, reported in the *American Journal of Psychiatry*, using statistics from the Swedish cause of death register, concluded that the rate of suicide was twice as high in families of suicide victims as in comparison families. Is it by example or genetic?

For years, researchers have tried to find a genetic marker for suicide. They haven't found it, but they have found evidence of a specific genetic link to suicidal behavior. In a 2000 study published in the *American Journal of Medical Genetics*, researchers found a mutation in a gene that regulates the brain's level of serotonin, a neurotransmitter that carries messages between brain cells and is thought to be involved in the regulation of emotion. They estimated that the mutation more than doubles the risk of suicidal behavior in those who have it.

The study was conducted at the Royal Ottawa Hospital. Psychiatrist David Bakish studied patients who could not stop thinking about suicide and who had a family history of suicide. "For some, suicide is a one-time cry for help," Bakish says. "But others simply can't control suicidal fantasies, nor can they stop themselves from attempting to take their own lives." This was the first study that compared brains from patients who had committed suicide to those who died by other means. Bakish and his team were looking at serotonin receptors. "We now know that each serotonin receptor is coded by a single gene," says Bakish. "What we found was that in patients who had committed suicide, they had 30 percent more of the specific serotonin receptor called the 5 HT 2 A receptor. If cells are not getting enough serotonin they build receptors in an attempt to soak up more. We found that there was some abnormality in the gene that codes for the receptor. What we did not know," he continues, "is whether over the course of time there was a change in the receptor because of environmental stressors or whether the abnormality was there when they were born."

"However, life is not so simple as just finding a gene," Bakish argues. "This is especially true as we learn more about genetics. We now know that over the course of time, environmental events can change the basic DNA. We call that science epigenetics. Therefore, ideally we should be following populations where we measured those genes at baseline and follow the patient over his lifetime to see if there are any changes. That of course is very difficult to do," he concedes.

If there is a genetic component to suicide, Bakish believes this finding could help families deal with the stigma of suicide. He is also hopeful that the discovery could lead to the development of genetic tests to identify those at risk to help prevent this kind of suffering.

But not all individuals who are at risk because of a family history of suicide, mental illness, or depression end their lives. Regardless of family history, according to varying statistical analysis approximately 80 to 90 percent of depressed or mentally ill people do not commit suicide. For instance, while it has been estimated that 90 percent of completed suicides of all

ages have a psychiatric disorder, more than 95 percent of people with psychiatric disorders do not take their lives. Although
clinicians have since recognized that many people who are not
depressed kill themselves, the National Health Care Quality
Report of 2003 asserts that 15 percent of depressed people will
commit suicide. "To reduce suicide to a biological basis is to
ignore the psychological pain which drives it," Edwin Shneidman has said. "There can be no pill that salves the human malaise that leads to suicide."

In spite of the literature on the genetic link to suicide, and
the commendable research on its behalf, I knew that I could
not categorize Kim's act as a mere product of her biology. Kay
Redfield Jamison, in her landmark work, *Night Falls Fast,* put
it most succinctly: "Genes are only part of the tangle of suicide,
but their clash with psychological and environmental elements
can prove to be the difference between life and death."

BRIGHT STAR

When I am writing about Kim she is here, sitting across from
me on the couch or next to me at my table. It's like that eerie
feeling when the moon passes through the earth's shadow after
an eclipse. I want to believe that she's at peace. That life on the
other side isn't so bad. That she's a bright star in its "still unrest," watching the world below her from high above, or that
like pollen in the air in spring, her essence is floating, ethereal
matter. Sometimes I find myself asking her why she had to leave
us, as if it were all plotted and planned and I will hear a convincing answer. Of course a part of me knows why. She felt as if she

had become a ghost in every room she entered, driving in her car on familiar roads, working the restaurant floor, at a party. And she did not want to play the part of a person who was un-encumbered anymore. When I remember her I'm content, but then the tide shifts and I have to say goodbye to her again.

WEDDING

I am home. It is October 1988, a year and a half before the hammer falls, and I am about to get married. All week we've been together, five women, my sisters, my mother, and me, full of wedding plans and arrangements. We get our hair done, our nails. We try on clothes in the bathroom, trade lipstick, perfume. The house is full of a feminine, earthy scent. And, for once, an air of celebration. Mom is reviewing the menu with the caterer, obsessing about the wedding cake; Cindy is reassuring me that the dress I've chosen to wear—ivory silk, just above the knee, with a lace skirt—is perfect; Laura is admiring my sapphire and diamond engagement ring; and Kim is happy. I see it in her eyes. "I love Dave," she tells me when we are in her room, talking on her bed. Everything, now that I've reached this threshold, seems full of possibility. "Are you nervous?" she asks me. I nod. I can see a sort of yearning in her eyes, but because I am about to begin what I've come to see as the first day of the rest of my life, I am certain the sadness will lift and that one day she'll be filled, as I thought I never would be, by the security of love. "Here, let me show you how to do your eyes," she tells me, taking out brown eyeliner and eye shadow from her makeup case, holding my chin in her hand. All that day and night we never once talk about her future, how things are going with Alan, how she likes school. We have all the rest of our days.

THE BODY CAN TOLERATE ONLY
SO MUCH KNOWLEDGE

There are things I don't want to know. Truths I want to keep buried. It's as if the body can tolerate only so much painful knowledge. When I was in New York focusing on my work as an editor and my writing, my newly married life, planning our dinners at night after work, our weekends, apartment shopping, I had imagined that one day, once Kim figured out what she wanted, she too would have these things. I suppose I didn't want to think about Kim struggling at home, and so I told myself that what she was going through was a natural part of growing up. I suppose there was a part of me that wanted to forget the world in Cleveland I had left behind.

In small increments, I allowed her death to possess me. It took me years to open the brown envelope my great aunt Harriet slipped into my hand after the seven days of shivah had passed and I was returning home to New York. Inside was a copy of Kim's suicide note and the obituary my other two sisters and I composed. (Somehow, in the middle of our shock and grief, we were able to maintain complete lucidity in composing her obituary. We three sisters sat around my mother's dining room table, and, as if we were putting together a menu and grocery list for a family dinner, we shaped into words the brief history of Kim's life.) Also in the envelope were copies of some of the childhood letters she had written to Aunt Harriet. I took the brown envelope and put it in my filing cabinet for safekeeping, for a day when I would feel strong enough to open it. For years I could not face reading anything intimately connected to Kim. It was too painful.

Then one day, two years later, I tore the apartment apart looking for that envelope. I was afraid that in losing the contents of the envelope, which in my mind had grown in importance, I'd lost the only concrete representation that she had existed, that she'd once sat in my lap, made me scrambled eggs, laughed at the odd things we thought funny. Also I was convinced that in one of those papers the enigma of her suicide might be explained. I could not find the envelope. It did not strike me as unusual that I might have misplaced it. But when it happened a second time, after Cindy had gone through the trouble of photocopying the same contents of the envelope from the one Aunt Harriet had given her, and this time I unconsciously misplaced it—again I remember bringing the envelope home and putting it in my filing cabinet for safekeeping—I saw how much I hadn't yet allowed myself to bring to the surface.

FIEND ANGELICAL

Who knew what demons lived in Alan's closet? To Kim, he was her "beautiful tyrant! Fiend angelical!" All I know is that things spun out of control. Perhaps Kim wanted more from Alan. She was no longer in touch with her own father. She believed he didn't care about her. Kim told me that, by then, he was with another woman, only a few years older than her.

He had divorced the woman for whom he left my mother. Kim told me he refused to pay for her tuition, help with her car payments or even her orthodontia bills, which seemed to have particularly upset her. Everything she owned came from money she'd saved working as a waitress. When she and Alan fought she often came back home to sleep, curling into her childhood bed still lined with her teddy bears and stuffed animals, angry and hurt that he didn't treat her better. Sometimes she cried until she could barely open her eyes. Kim struggled with her feelings for him. Surely she must have had dialogues with herself filled with sophisticated arguments about the wrongs he had done, working herself up to leaving him. She was wrestling with something essentially flawed and unfair that had to do with men, though without knowing exactly how to articulate or understand it. How he could rule over her emotions, make her sick, and how after hours of fighting with herself, determined never to let him set foot in her house again, he would flash her one of his sad, I-need-you looks and, stuffing down her hurt, she went back to him again.

She was coming home a little buzzed or high to escape her longing, hoping she could save him. She slept into the afternoon, caught in an awful cycle: after that warm rush of the first drink she felt better but then the self-flagellation followed, hating herself because she was sick and hungover and had lost another day, maybe two, and then partying again to escape the punishing voices in her head. I imagine that after the first snort of white powder, she was filled with adrenaline, that secret rush, until she awoke listless the next day, her head blank, as if she were already leading a posthumous existence.

Like Kim's father, Alan knew the sly art of winning her back: buying her presents, taking her out to nice dinners. He knew how to make her feel she was needed once he found he had trouble waking up without her; he knew how to reel her back in. After a while Kim stopped talking about him or their problems because the only acceptable response was to ask why she didn't leave him—and she couldn't. At least not then. At that age, I too had struggled with letting go of an unhealthy attachment. I told myself it needed to run its course.

Not long after, when they'd gotten back together, the tension reached its height. Maybe Alan was jealous that she was trying to better herself by going to college, or perhaps he saw her at the bar talking to another guy. Maybe she said something that flipped a switch inside him. I only know that she came home with her face smashed, her eyes so bruised she couldn't open them. My mother took her to the emergency room. For the weeks when her face was healing from the bruises and puffiness she vowed she wouldn't see him again. "He's fucked up," she said, trying to explain what he'd done. "His mother is crazy. He has no one." When she moved back home, our mother was relieved. To cheer Kim up, she brought home their favorite ice cream sundae from Draeger's called Marvin's Mistake: one scoop vanilla ice cream, one scoop chocolate, hot fudge, marshmallow sauce, whipped cream, and a sprinkle of nuts topped with a cherry.

But eventually the long, torturous, all-night phone calls started and she struggled with whether to go back to him. Even when she moved out of his house he was still under her skin, as if he possessed her. In trying to understand her own contradictory behavior, wrestling with her doubts, doing homework for composition class, her emotions evolved into an essay she composed called "TRUST":

> *The most important part to any relationship, is trust. If you can't trust somebody, then there is no possible way to really care about them. It doesn't matter if it is your mother, a friend, a relative, or a boyfriend. Trust is important in any relationship. If somebody lies to you, it could get you into trouble, it could hurt somebody else, and it could just hurt you.*
>
> *Honesty is so important. It feels so bad when somebody lies to you. It is just like being betrayed. If you care about someone, then you don't expect them to lie to you ever. When they do, you not only feel betrayed, you feel stupid. You are mad at yourself for ever believing in them in the first place. It is a really hard thing to get over.*
>
> *Then there is always the question of giving somebody another chance. They have already told you lies before, but they think that they deserve to be trusted. They promise it will never happen again. I have a real hard time with that line. If they have done it once, there is no question in my mind that that person will do it again.*
>
> *I've been told that I am too sensitive. That everyone has to lie once in a while. I just don't think that somebody you care about should lie to you, no matter what the circumstances are. Maybe I am too trusting. I always trust a person until they give me a reason not to. That is probably a dumb thing to do, but that is just how I am.*

Slowly, taking classes in college, challenging her intellect, writing about herself, she was coming into her own. But though her writing showed glimpses of awakening self-awareness and the sense of pride she felt about going back to school, she lacked the confidence and foresight to see it through. What was more important to a twenty-year-old girl full of yearning: bettering herself for an unknown future or the security of love in the here and now? Sometimes it must have been enough to be out of the house sitting across from him on a blanket spread out on the lake's beach and have him look into her eyes. To go out for pizza and a pitcher of beer and come back to his house with the purring kittens rubbing against her ankles. It must have been enough in the morning to go with him to the diner and sit at the counter and have eggs and hash browns for breakfast to soak up last night's buzz. But what were these individual moments amounting to? I doubt that he was giving her much pleasure. Yet what was her choice: to leave him and be left with no one?

I wish I could describe how beautiful Kim was. I have tried. Thick, long blond hair, blue eyes, hourglass figure, and a twinkling, innocent smile. When I think about her I still see her child's face in the beautiful woman she was becoming. She was two people. The young, beautiful blond girl who wore pink stretch pants with Bugs Bunny on her sweatshirt and black lace lingerie underneath. She was tender and tough, lovable and distant, childlike and sexy. She could have had anyone, but she did not have the confidence. In her last year she vacillated between giving in to her need for Alan and seeking refuge from him with my mother, unable to leave either of them. When she had a fight with Alan she returned to my mother's house, and when she felt suffocated by my mother she returned to Alan.

I learned in my research that not being able to separate from someone who is perpetuating physical and emotional abuse is recognized as a psychological disorder in the *DSM-IV Diagnos-*

tic and Statistical Manual of Mental Disorders. It is considered pathological and is characterized by "over reliance on others that leads to submissive and clinging behavior." Psychiatrist Samuel Klagsbrun believes that if an adolescent has no other sources of self-esteem, the relationship becomes exceedingly overvalued. Those who are overly dependent are at greater risk for depression, alcohol or drug abuse, and emotional, physical, or sexual abuse. Overdependence can inhibit one's ability to form healthy relationships, finish school, find satisfying work, and develop the sustained confidence to construct an independent life.

In her last year Kim struggled with building an independent life. In a journal entry for composition class dated May 3, 1988, Kim wrote about spending some time at her best friend's house. She conveyed the innocence of enjoying the company of her friends, but her writing also revealed the way in which she viewed her brief experience living away from home and her ambivalence about returning:

> *I really can't wait until Thursday. I have a friend named Mary and we have been friends since we were like five or so. When we were in the fifth grade we somehow got our mothers together, and they have been best friends ever since. Anyways, Mary's mom is going to go to New York on Thursday for about ten days. She thinks it would be a good thing for me to stay with Mary, because I "have experience living on my own," as she puts it. Mary and I find this very funny. I would have stayed there even if her mom did not ask me to. I really am anxious to go there. It will be nice to get out of my mom's house for a week. (I live at home again. My so-called experience away from home wasn't a very good one.)*

Anyways, Mary and I get along great. We hardly ever argue or have disagreements. We are going to have a blast next week. Last time my mom went out of town for three weeks. That was almost two years ago in July. It was the first summer that all my friends were home from college, and eight girls lived in my house for three weeks. Probably the best three weeks of all of our lives. Or at least the most eventful. Just because I said there were eight girls that lived there doesn't mean that that is the only people that were there. It was a constant madhouse. People coming and going all the time. I'm not trying to give the impression that we just partied or anything the whole time because we didn't. I am not a big partier, or wasn't then at least. Lots of times we just had dates over and cooked fancy dinners. We would all dress very formal and sit down in our dining room and have a very fancy meal. We used to get drunk from wine or champagne so I guess we did party a lot but in a classier way than the average eighteen year old.

I think it is going to be a lot of fun to spend some time with Mary. I'm sure she will have to have at least one party because that is how Mary is. She always wants to have fun. I'm sure she will.

Kim's teacher wrote at the bottom of her paper: "What do you think about living on your own?"

BEACH II

I am at the beach. It has been raining for eighteen days, but on the horizon there is a sliver of blue sky and beneath the cumulous the sun is threatening to break through. For a second it does and for that moment everything is bright and clear, the water sparkling, the blue band of sky widening on the horizon.

A group of teenagers has wandered down the beach. They run close to the surf and then back again, yelling and chasing one another, until eventually, tired, they settle on a blanket nearby. I overhear that they are new graduates. Among them are three girls with long hair, wearing tight blue jeans and little T-shirts and zippered sweatshirts. I can smell their perfume and shampoo on the breeze. There are four boys, clean-cut, barefoot, wearing colored collared shirts and Livestrong bracelets on their wrists. Nice kids, I think to myself. I imagine that by now they have money in their pockets, know how to read train schedules, how to get from one place to another. They can drive. Soon they will find summer internships in the city or go on to college. Who in the bunch might falter? Who among them might need medication for loneliness, require too many beers or joints to keep the darkness at bay? Who would prefer to be in the arms of another, no matter the consequences, rather than walk alone? Who among them, confident, buoyed by making the honor roll, or playing varsity soccer, or getting the lead in the school play, is on their way to fulfill a dream?

part five

GROUP

For the first time, I want to connect to others who have lost family members to suicide. I wonder whether my strange, confusing, and private journey to understand Kim's suicide is similar to ones others have experienced. And so, nearly two decades after Kim's death, I begin attending a monthly bereavement group for survivors of suicides. The psychologist who leads the group lost her mother to suicide when she was a baby. Her practice and life course seem to be fueled by her mother's act. One of the other group leaders had a sister who ended her life.

We sit in a small, white-walled room on black folding chairs in an office building on lower Fifth Avenue, strangers to one another, veterans of suicide in a world of mostly civilians. The meeting begins as we go around in a circle introducing ourselves and the person we have lost to suicide: brothers, sisters, sons, daughters, mothers, fathers, wives, lovers, best friends. No matter what the relationship of the speaker is to the lost, no matter how many weeks or years have passed, there is still the same pained and bewildered look in the face of the participant. There is no simple way to explain why a person's will gave out, nor any timeline for understanding or acceptance.

At the first meeting there is a man in his late sixties, hands

uncomfortably pressed into his pockets as he talks, still mourning the suicide of his father when he was eight. Beside him is a
young man in his early thirties wearing blue jeans and a black
T-shirt with his wife's name tattooed on his forearm, grieving
over her suicide just three months earlier. Both of these men,
separated by generations, are as bewildered by suicide as the
rest of us in this room so quiet you can hear someone unwrap-
ping paper from a cough drop. I quickly come to see that my
unwieldy experience has been no different from the others;
there is no map to follow when faced with the kind of loss and
grief a suicide provokes. Human nature is mysterious. How are
we to know why at one moment someone's anguish is so overwhelming she can't get out of bed? Why on the next day that
same person seems to have found the spark of life again? Why
on one day the world appears to hold endless possibilities and
on another day taking a shower feels like an effort? How are we
to understand why someone we feel we know intimately would
end her life when we cannot at times fathom our own natures?
What if I had walked into the house I grew up in just as Kim
was contemplating her death? Would my presence that day have
forestalled her suicide? Is our fate governed by random acts
or determined by our histories? The man who lost his father
to suicide when he was a child comes forward. "Time doesn't
really heal," he says. "It only makes living more bearable."

The first time I attend the monthly group I am uncertain if I
belong. But I soon discover there are two sets of people present: those who have lost someone to suicide within the past
year and those, like me, who have been survivors for years or
even decades. I am comforted to know I am not the only one

who has not been able to reconcile my emotions. In the psychological reading I have done about grief, mine was considered "complicated." "In complicated grief, painful emotions are so long lasting and severe that you have trouble accepting the death and resuming your own life," according to the Mayo Clinic's website. But how could mourning a suicide not be complicated? When I look at those newly grieving I want to say, Don't worry, it feels like you won't be able to get past the pain and suffering but you'll get used to it. I am slightly jaded and uncomfortable. I'm not a group person and something about the confessional nature of the group experience makes me uneasy. But then a young woman begins to speak. She wraps a protective scarf three or four times around her neck as she tells the story about her boyfriend, who shot himself. "He was in a bad place," she says, "but I never thought he'd do this. Why didn't I see it? Why couldn't he pull through?" And the shell begins to crack just slightly and it is as if Kim has died only yesterday. Each time I leave group I tell myself I won't be coming back, but then it's the beginning of the month, the first Friday, and I find myself sitting in the stiff black chair, Kleenex bunched in my hand, comforted by being with strangers who share the same hollow ache.

Bearing witness to the suffering in the enclosed room pushes me to dig deeper and try to uncover the vulnerable tendrils of the unconscious to explore Kim's last weeks and days.

SECRET LIFE

I picture Kim sitting by the sofa near the window at home, where she returned to put some distance between herself and

Alan. In search of solace, back in our mother's house, she might have watched the cars cross the intersection and the forsythia newly in bloom, dreaming of a life beyond the corner as the clock continued to tick forward.

When our mother was in a good period, when her zest for life had come back and she could put aside her worries and anxieties, it seemed like the world had tilted and suddenly what was once dark brightened. I remember I used to feel happy seeing my mother scramble a skillet of eggs. She took on projects, like fixing up the house, or went flea-marketing with her friends where she collected old postcards and Fiestaware. She made grand dinners on holidays and birthdays. She worked in an upscale clothing store, where she took pride in helping customers find the perfect outfit. She liked nothing more than to put aside clothes from the store she thought her daughters would like when we came home to visit. Her energy was infectious. Once Oprah was running some kind of Mother's Day promotion. Viewers were to send in cards saying why they thought their mother was the best mother in the world. The winner would get a free trip somewhere, a chance to be on *Oprah,* and some cash. Kim sent in an entry and our mother, full of pride, told me about it. But when Kim moved back home the last time, my mother's disposition was dark. She wasn't working; years before, she'd gotten her real estate license and had sold a few houses, but perhaps due to lack of confidence or a dry spell in the market she'd let her license expire. It was as if her mood had worsened from situational malaise into a despair that seemed to have headed into full-fledged depression.

Sometimes depression seemed to wrap my mother in its dark robe and steal her away. She felt trapped inside, unable to understand depression's repercussions on others and unable to see beyond its confines. She stayed home all day when she suffered migraines, sometimes with the blinds down because any light was too painful. She had her up periods and her down periods, but no matter what we did to try to encourage her, her malaise overpowered her good intentions. My sisters and I, including Kim, talked about her constantly. We were worried and didn't know what to do.

We all thought it was our mother's situation—a widow and divorcee with little financial means, four children, no husband—and not an illness that was at the bottom of her melancholy. At that time, in the 1970s and '80s, the devastation that depression inflicts on an individual and a family was not widely recognized. Even today it is poorly understood and, because of individual complexities, can be inadequately treated as an illness. It continues to perplex me.

I have often wondered whether my mother's depression began long ago when her mother died. She seemed to be in a perpetual state of mourning for a life that had been snatched from her first when she was a nine-year-old child and lost her mother and then again when she lost her husband in her early twenties. In periods of despair, her mourning, left untreated, turned her melancholic, as her inner world grew private and secret.

"Why can't you make yourself happy?" my mother told me Kim used to ask her. I worried that Kim, living alone with our mother, felt she shouldered the burden. Our mother was in her early fifties, still youthful looking, but she had little confidence in finding gainful employment. In the secluded suburbs of Cleveland there were few opportunities to find a well-paying job for women her age without a college education or experience. She lived off alimony checks and near the end of each month grew anxious when the bills stacked up. She was lonely for male companionship and sometimes dated again, hoping to find happiness, but when the dates proved disappointing, she retreated back inside the insular world of the house, consumed by crippling inertia and head-splitting migraines.

"Mom, why don't you find a new job?" Kim asked. We all encouraged our mother. I can see Kim in a long T-shirt, bare-legged, having just woken up, wandering into the kitchen to find my mother making a cup of tea. "No one wants me," my mother often said. It was one of her common refrains. "That's your excuse," Kim might have replied, sucking in her abdomen as she sometimes did when she caught her reflection in the full-length mirror my mother had tacked on the refrigerator door. "Don't worry, honey," my mother said, as she so often did, not wanting us to worry, as she crossed off another day from the Calendar of Phrases on the corkboard. I always liked the collection of phrases she pasted there, some cutouts she found from the paper or other sayings she had written out. This was where I first discovered Sartre's "As far as men go, it is not what they are that interests me, but what they can become," or Albert Einstein's "Imagination is more important than knowledge."

"Something will happen," my mother often reassured Kim.

"Not unless you make it happen," Kim said, or rolled her eyes, or turned away. What Kim wanted was simple: a house with a protective fence around it and sun shining through all the fence rows, confidence, someone to love her.

My mother told me that sometimes she heard Kim crying in her room after she'd broken up with Alan. My mother tried

to comfort her. "I'm OK, Mom," she told me Kim said, struggling to smile, puzzled no doubt by the weight of her unhappiness. They ordered in a late-night pizza or watched a movie
together, wearing the same sweatshirts and sweaters. When the
pain in Kim's chest got so bad that she did not know how to
make herself stop crying, she'd climb upstairs to sleep next to
my mother in her bed.

"Don't you know how guilty I feel about that?" my mother
says on the eighteen-year anniversary of Kim's death, in reference to her own inability to make herself happy or see outside the fog of her depression. "I can't believe all the mistakes
I made. I didn't know I was doing anything wrong. When you
get older you figure it out. It's awful."

I remember years ago watching a movie called *The Bear* one
Sunday morning on the nature channel. Lucas was four or five
then. In the film the mother bear was wounded. The baby bear
circled his mother helplessly, the agony in her movements palpable. He tentatively approached the mother bear, licked his
mother's wound, backed away, anxious and agitated. Then he
moved toward his mother and began licking her wound again.
The mother bear licked her cub's face. Their interaction portrayed the primal instinct of attachment. Lucas leapt off my
lap and moved toward the door. "I can't watch," he said. He
half hid his eyes and half looked back at the television. "What
happens if the mother bear dies? Who will take care of him?"

Enmeshment is a psychodynamic term that describes the state
of being from which all children must wrest their sense of in-

dividual selfhood. Psychologists Mahler, Pine, and Bergman argue in *The Psychologcial Birth of the Human Infant* that when children are born, they experience themselves as part of a symbiotic relationship with their mothers. As a child develops, she begins to see that her mother is a separate being with her own thoughts and feelings. However, an emotionally deprived and depressed mother may feel threatened by her child's growing separation and unconsciously promote the enmeshment. The consequences can be severe, interfering with the child's ability to assert a separate identity. Preoccupied with worries about her mother's survival, a child is deprived not only of a childhood but also of the chance to develop a healthy sense of her own self, apart from her mother. And what happens when that child is suddenly faced with responsibility in school, in society, in the outside world, but does not yet have the inner strength and resources? Anna Freud, daughter of Sigmund Freud and founder of child psychoanalysis, said that some children "follow the mother into depression."

During this period, when Kim had taken a semester break from Cleveland State her sophomore year and was living back at home, she contemplated, in one of her brief surges of optimism, taking a course at the local community college. My mother said that maybe she would, too. Kim quickly decided against it. It was complicated. She was struggling to put some distance between herself and our mother and yet at the same time depended on her for emotional support. We three sisters, worried about their interdependence, tried to convince her to go away to college. Cindy and I had gone to Ohio University; we encouraged her to apply and offered to take her to visit the campus. For a moment there was a sparkle in her eye, as if she were considering a life beyond the circumference of the familiar neighborhood, but then something inside made her decide against it. Perhaps she was too enmeshed in our mother and their circumstance to make a move. "I'm going to finish here," she replied, pulling a strand of hair back behind her ear. "I'm going back next semester. Come here, Gretel," she said, coaxing her cat onto her lap. "You love me, don't you, Grettie," she said, rubbing her face into Gretel's soft black coat.

In one of the papers Kim wrote for a college composition course, she described an awareness she had gained about herself from a novel I had given her that year for Christmas. Dated April 25, 1988, the essay begins:

> I have just read a book titled "Anywhere But Here," by Mona Simpson. The story is about a girl who grows up with her mother. The father has left and the mother is kind of strange. It is a really nice story, and is one of the first books that I've read that has made me think about my childhood a lot.
>
> The story starts out with the little girl, her name is Ann, really worshipping her mother. She is too young to realize that the things her mother has her do are wrong. Ann is growing up very unhappy and confused and she believes that it is her own fault. It is really her mother that is making her unhappy. Being very disturbed herself, the mother takes many of her own problems out on Ann. Anything Ann does well, her mother shoots down. She tries so hard to please her mother, it is an impossible thing to do.

When she grows a little older, Ann starts to realize that her mother really does have problems of her own. She sees that she is going to have to concentrate on herself. She loves her mother but she knows that she is going to have to control her future all by herself.

Reading this story, I thought about myself. It kind of made me learn that my mother's problems are hers, not mine. She is old enough to solve them by herself. I need to focus on my life. I need to find my own direction. It is time for me to take charge of my life. I can't live my mother's for her, and she can't live mine.

Her teacher wrote in the margin: "Sounds like a very important step in becoming an adult."

I think of lines from "Symptoms," a poem that Robert Lowell, a victim of bipolar disease, wrote about his despair, imagining that he was in a bath (lake of the grave) without a mother to pull him out. When Lowell suffered his fatal heart attack at sixty, his third wife called it a "suicide wish."

> . . . life-enhancing water brims my bath—
> (the bag of waters or the lake of the grave . . . ?)
> from the palms of my feet to my wet neck—
> I have no mother to lift me in her arms.

Perhaps my mother was able to sustain herself through her dark times by creating a hazy world of dreams and fantasies for a future in which everything would eventually work out, even if she didn't quite believe it. It was a coping mechanism that seemed to keep her afloat while paradoxically her daughter, lying on her bed, staring at the ceiling, may have felt—even unconsciously inherited, if we do indeed inherit emotional states—some of the pain, hopelessness, and insecurities our mother was trying to deny or overcome.

Psychoanalyst Adam Phillips argues that when we don't have a narrative for our despair, we can't rid ourselves of, or change or redefine, it. "So it is as though, from a psychoanalytic point of view, our unbearable self-knowledge leads a secret life: as though there is self-knowledge, but not for us."

PIGEONS

Laura and I are sitting at an outdoor garden café somewhere in the East Village having a glass of white wine and a bite to eat. We are talking about Kim, as we periodically do, especially close to the anniversary of her death, each trying to shed some new light on the culmination of events that caused our sister to take her life. "I still can't believe it," I say. Laura says that as few years as we had with our father, we were brought into the world feeling secure and loved. We were formed in whole cloth. Kim, on the other hand, was born into an environment of insecurity and instability. "But she was happy," I say. "When she was a baby and a young girl. We all adored her. Why wasn't it enough to sustain her?" As we are talking a pigeon swoops down and begins to flutter around our table, flapping its excitable gray wings. "It caught up to her," Laura says. Then the pigeon flies back again, its ruffling wings touching my hair. Both Laura and I look at each other with the same thought. Why is the pigeon only hovering over our table? "She's trying to tell us something," Laura says. "She's OK."

WHEN DARKNESS FALLS

In his best-selling classic about his battle with depression, *Darkness Visible,* William Styron describes the "downward spiral of depression" that overcame him as he approached sixty and how suicide became in his mind the only way to escape his anguish. This depression, he speculates, was triggered by years of alcohol abuse and during the "manifest crisis" by the overuse of the sleeping pill Halcyon. Remarkably, it is only in the last pages of his memoir, after his depression has lifted and he is beyond its debilitation, that he realizes that the depression began long ago, when, at the age of twelve, he lost his mother.

Inadequate or unresolved grieving finally caught up with Styron at the age of sixty; his dependency on alcohol during his adulthood may have distanced him from his loss and feelings of childhood abandonment. Styron writes, "Incomplete mourning has validity . . . and it is also true that in the nethermost depths of suicidal behavior one is still subconsciously dealing with immense loss while trying to surmount all the effects of its devastation."

The underlying roots of depression often reside in unresolved, unprocessed traumatic events in childhood. In understanding the onslaught of his depression, Styron writes that the triggering events interested him less than the earlier origins of the disease. "What are the forgotten or buried events that suggest an ultimate explanation for the evolution of depression and its later flowering into madness?" he writes. "After I returned to health and was able to reflect on the past in the light of my ordeal, I began to see clearly how depression had clung close to the outer edges of my life for many years." In his memoir, Styron pens insights from historian Howard I. Kushner's book on suicide, *Self-Destruction in the Promised Land.* Kushner makes a convincing case "not only for the idea of early loss precipitating self-destructive conduct, but also, auspiciously, for that same behavior becoming a strategy through which the person involved comes to grips with his guilt and rage, and triumphs over self-willed death."

We cannot always know exactly what losses or hurts will stay with those we love or even with us, nor which losses and hurts we might or might not overcome. Perhaps because no parent can truly accept the notion that his or her own child has been harmed and is suffering emotional distress so severe she will die by her own hand, signs of suicidal thoughts and behavior can often go undetected. Studies show that parents are unaware of 90 percent of suicide attempts made by their teenagers. "They aren't intentionally missed, but unknowingly missed," states psychiatrist Andrew Slaby. Our mechanisms of denial often prevent us from comprehending the severity of another person's emotional and psychic anguish. Children or young adults, even adults, rarely have the emotional distance or knowledge to understand their own anguish. Of our inability to know ourselves, philosopher and psychoanalyst Allen Wheelis writes:

We tend to assume that we know what we are, that our nature is obvious, given to us by direct observation of others and of ourselves: Just look around the world and look into your own heart and you will know the human condition. It's not so. What it is to be a human being is not clear at all, but deeply shrouded. Because, in the evolution from animal life to human life, along with the gain in knowledge and awareness, we have gained also the ability to deceive ourselves. We arrange not to know our nature, and not to see what we are up to. Our self-deceptions are so dense, piled on so thick . . . that it is all but impossible to break through, to get a clear view of what we really are.

Is it our unknowability that finally makes suicide an enigma? Perhaps, as Edwin Shneidman says, "the greatest fallacy about suicide lies in the belief that there is a single immediate answer—or perhaps combined answers—as to why the deed was done."

HOPELESSNESS

Depression alone does not explain suicide. Though depression and suicide are closely linked, for every teenage suicide there are hundreds of depressed teenagers, argues George Howe Colt in *November of the Soul: The Enigma of Suicide*. Colt writes that "clinicians have struggled to isolate the factors that separate suicidal depression from depression, but to explain the differences they tend to come up with abstractions such as 'loneliness,' 'isolation,' 'low self-esteem,' and a profound sense of 'worthlessness.'" He cites psychiatrist Aaron Beck, the founder of cognitive therapy. Beck believes "hopelessness" is the key factor, and a series of studies have shown it to be a key predictor of suicide in depressed patients.

Beck measured three major aspects of hopelessness: feelings about the future, loss of motivation, and expectations. Hopelessness refers to the individual's conviction that conditions will never improve, that there is no solution to a problem, and "for many, a feeling that dying by suicide would be better than living."

Young people who feel hopeless need help in solving problems and think their parents often don't understand or are not involved enough to know the depth of their need. Objectively they do not have more problems than others, but they are less equipped to deal with them. People are able to tolerate depression as long as there is a feeling that things will improve. If that belief is shattered the only option may be suicide.

William Styron writes, "It is hopelessness even more than pain that crushes the soul." He describes hopelessness as "moving from pain to pain. One does not abandon, even briefly, one's bed of nails, but is attached to it wherever it goes."

In trying to understand why Kim's strength gave out, I muse over why certain people can be depressed, even chronically depressed, and never become so hopeless that they feel they need to end their lives. For some, severe depression can drain the energy to carry out the act. But perhaps for the suicide, in that moment of resignation, the "super ego"—which Freud described as the aspects of the personality composed of our internalized ideals we have acquired from our parents and society—is more combative, unwilling to allow the self to live an untenable existence.

In most cases of depression there is a degree of hopelessness, but in a suicidal person it has reached rock bottom. But there are people who seem habitually hopeless and are either not suicidal or are chronically suicidal in a manner that is more symbolic and not truly lethal. It is mysterious as to why some tolerate this state and others cannot. "This touches on one of the great questions of psychiatric illness, which is framed in different ways: why does the same event/illness/stress break some people while not breaking others?" says Dr. George Makari of the Weill Cornell Medical College.

A friend I met recently who lost his thirty-three-year-old brother to suicide talks about it like this. "Do you know when you accidentally touch a hot kettle on the stove, your body reacts and you instantly, without thinking, move your hand? The way I see it, for my brother the inner pain was so bad that instinctively he couldn't protect himself. Our bodies want nothing more than to live. The darkness your sister and my brother lived within prevents that protection."

Dr. Lanny Berman, executive director of the American Association of Suicidology, says research suggests that about a quarter of suicides are impulsive: the idea strikes and the person acts quickly. I wonder about the link between hopelessness and impulsivity. "We just don't know enough about the relationship between the thoughts and the behavior," Dr. Berman said. "People who are thinking about it more often than not talk themselves out of the act, also on a sudden whim."

WHY, WHY, WHY

Another month goes by and I attend again the monthly drop-in suicide bereavement group. I sit in a chair in the semicircle of the room filled with strangers who, because of our shared loss, I feel connected to, though I know very little about their daily lives, where they work, go to school, live. I consider, as I listen to the stories told that day, whether the need to talk about the events that led up to the suicide is an attempt to control the internal chaos it provokes. Or is it guilt that compels us? Or fear that if we do not locate the time and place, the exact moment along the way where our loved one became unhinged, someone else we love will end his or her life and once again we'll be blindsided?

In the white room where we meet once a month, sealed off from the cacophony of traffic on the avenue below us—pedestrians heading home from work, lovers walking arm in arm—the litany of *what ifs* and *why didn't I* and *if only* rises like a chorus of voices in a Greek tragedy. As I listen to the stories about those who suffered and ended their lives it seems to me that it isn't as if they wanted to die, but more that they wished to feel better and didn't know how.

A young woman who has lost her older brother to suicide tells her story. She is a beautiful Latina wearing a colorful scarf around her head and bracelets that bang against each other when she lifts her hands to speak. "I have no one," she says. "I'm all alone. It's because of what he did." Her brother ended his life his senior year of high school. She was three years younger. "I'm afraid to love anyone," she says. She describes her brother and then suicides in general as people with a switch inside, a mechanism that he or she switches on and "boom, it's over." She describes her brother as someone who had a lower threshold for emotional pain. "He was brilliant, beautiful, smart," she says. "He had gotten a DWI and he was afraid to tell my parents. Didn't he know that he was leaving me all alone? Son of a bitch. Motherfucker."

A woman with a thick Boston accent has lost a friend to suicide just a few months ago, a man she has known since high school. She is baffled. She describes the feeling of disbelief almost as though she's in one of those rides at the amusement park and suddenly the floor drops. She says her entire life view is shaken. She can't figure out what would have made him take his life. She says he had no problems with addiction, loss of work, illness. He was married and seemed to love his wife. He was a sixty-three-year-old man who went into his bedroom and hung himself, and no one knows why. Another girl in her twenties mourns her best friend. "We were like sisters," she says. "Why?" And I think to myself, listening to these people, strangers, all of us from different walks of life, that no matter the cause of the suicide, we are linked by our pain and disbelief. Could it be as simple as a switch? Could it be that on that day and maybe that day only, she or he couldn't take it anymore? And all along I thought if only I could trace the little bread crumbs that Kim left in her wake and connect them, I would understand.

The nature of suicide—*I want to die and be done with life*—speaks to the paradoxes of human nature and perhaps that is why it frightens us. Each time I have mentioned to someone that my sister committed suicide I have observed nearly the same look pass across my companion's face: a wave first of shock, then disbelief, fear, and compassion. Sometimes there is discomfort or the desire to flee.

"The hardest part is that no one seems to understand," says the schoolteacher in her early twenties, dressed in blue jeans and a Gap hooded sweatshirt, who has lost her best friend to suicide. "I go about my day but I'm weighed down. Everyone thinks I should be over it by now. They want me to go out and party with them, but I'm different now. I see the world differently. I hear Nan call out to me and I still want to save her."

Once a suicide occurs, the unanswered and shattering questions—how essential we are to another human being and yet, at times, damaging in spite of our best efforts—are raised. We think we understand the people who are close to us. But do we? In defining the difference between characters in life and in fiction, E. M. Forster writes perceptively about the unknowable self:

> For human intercourse, as soon as we look at it for its own sake and not as a social adjunct, is seen to be haunted by a spectre. We cannot understand each other, except in a rough and ready way; we cannot reveal ourselves, even when we want to; what we call intimacy is only a makeshift; perfect knowledge is an illusion.

Or is it perhaps more simply that the more desperate we are, the more alone we become, and the more unknowable to others and ourselves?

As I walk down the silent corridor after group, thinking about the stories told that evening, it is as though I've been in a wood, a deep and tangled thicket, and then slowly things begin to clear. When a suicide occurs, the focus of any investigation is generally on the most recent state of mind of the deceased rather than on the personal history, childhood events, and circumstances that preceded and compounded the suicidal state. But the suicidal thoughts may coalesce over time, the way a stream does, gathering momentum as disappointments in the present tap into hurts from the past. It cannot be dismissed as predetermined, genetically based, or circumstantial. It is more complicated. The reason Kim chose to end her life may be no different from why our next-door neighbor's daughter ended hers, or every beloved mourned in group, or Sylvia Plath, or the poet Charlotte Mew. Or my friend Chris, whose slow addiction to drugs and eventual overdose was his own suicide. Suicides do not end their lives because they are weak, mentally ill, or depressed—though certainly they may be all those things. They are in blinding, all-consuming psychic pain, and perhaps on that final poisonous day they can find no reason not to.

After group, when we are in the elevator and preparing to walk back into the world of civilians, I look at the young schoolteacher in the Gap sweatshirt and nod. That is how we say goodbye. But as we walk out of the elevator together, then out the doors of the building onto the street, we pause, face each other, as if there is more we want to say, and then we look at each other again and shake our heads. "It didn't have to happen," she says to me, as if she'd read my mind.

MEDEA

While I am immersed in writing about Kim, I have coffee with a friend of mine, a poet who has translated some of Euripides's plays. He lost his father and his uncle to suicide, and the ways in which suicide has shaped our lives are the backstory to many of our conversations. "How much does family have to do with it?" I ask him.

"Think about Medea if you want to think about the effect of parents on their children. Medea was the mother of all mothers," he says, and we laugh.

Medea shows how the fates of children are inevitably tied to the deeds of their parents. After Medea and her husband, Jason, have had several children, Jason betrays her by announcing his intention to marry Glauce, the daughter of Creon. He tells Medea that this marriage to Glauce is for their mutual gain, a means to greater political power. Medea doesn't believe him and, seeking revenge, poisons Glauce. When the deed is discovered, Medea murders her own children out of fear that they will be killed for her actions. Medea's motherly devotion has become twisted by her own overwhelming and unfulfilled desires.

As with Medea and Jason, the actions and misdeeds of parents, whether purposeful or not, affect their children. When looking for an explanation for human tragedy and the importance of leading a conscious life, one can always draw parallels with the Greek stories, and that is why they endure, so we can try to explain our own tragedies even when no one explanation holds for long.

GROUP II

A new woman has come to group this month. She is in her early thirties, thin and curvy with long wavy hair, someone you might see on the street and admire how well she's put together. On her finger is a shiny diamond ring. There is no identifying mark on her body to indicate she's suffered a tragedy, though as I look more closely at her, I notice she has a twitch in her eyes that makes her unable to stop blinking for any period of time. She comes late and apologizes. We've already gone around the room and introduced ourselves, told our brief stories about those we have lost to suicide. "I don't know why I'm here," she begins. "I'm not really a group person. My older brother hung himself four months ago. He was forty. He was the second suicide in my family. We had a younger brother. He hung himself when he was ten. My parents never told us it was a suicide but I always knew. My older brother killed himself the same way. I think he was trying to get our parents to wake up." Then she looks around the room and puts her hand to her mouth, struck by the truth she's vocalized. "For days, weeks, I think I'm fine and then I find myself unable to stop crying," she says. "I'm afraid my husband is going to divorce me if he keeps seeing me fall apart."

Throughout the hour and a half in which we are together—Caucasian, Chinese, Latino, and African American—I notice that I can't stop staring at this woman, as if I'm drawn to her in some way I can't articulate. And then it occurs to me that when Kim died, I was approximately the age she is now, in my early thirties, newly married, trying to begin my life, attempting not to fall apart.

BEACH III

"Did you know she was sad, Mom?" Lucas asks. I look at him and nod. "But not as sad as she must have been," I say. It is February holiday from school and we are out at our house near the beach. It's cold and windy and I want to take a walk on the beach and he is resisting. I tell him how lucky we are to be close to the sea. "What do you like about the beach so much, Mom?" he asks.

"It connects me to the other world," I tell him. "When I'm by the sea I feel connected to Kim. It's where I go when I want to think about her. Do you believe in something beyond this life?" I ask him. "I don't believe in God," he says, a little cocky, like it's cool not to believe in anything. "I want you to believe in something," I tell him, and give him my little speech about faith and how important it is to believe in a power outside us. How sometimes in life we come to a crossroads where the world feels dark and empty and we are alone and frightened and it is good to have faith. "Right, Mom," he says, adopting his father's sardonic humor, but I know he's listening. We get out of the car. The wind is fierce, the sky an amazing blue. The waves are crashing so loudly we can't hear each other talk. We begin to walk down to the sea and the strength of the wind, whipping and twisting our clothes against us, makes it nearly impossible. Still I insist that we walk. Later, as we return to where we began, he tugs my arm affectionately. "Did you make your connection, Mom?" he asks. I nod. "Good," he says. "Now can we go?"

FAITH

Faith. What is it? How does it keep us from sinking into despair? Or is it our intimate connections and community that sustain us? And where, in modern life, do we go to seek places of comfort and solace?

Occasionally, I find myself going into the synagogue where we belong on my way home from work. I sit on the bench and look at the bema.

I want to tell Kim things. I want to tell her that Mom's been weeding in the garden and is taking a painting class. I want to tell her that Lucas is on a tournament baseball team and plays second base. I want to tell her about a certain book I read that I liked because she loved to read novels, or recant a story about Cindy or Laura. I miss catching a glimpse of the world as she would have seen it if she were still alive and with me. After a few minutes I get up and leave. Is it an act of faith that brings me to the synagogue, or simply a need to connect my voice to Kim's? I am not sure.

Before Kim was born my sisters and I went to the same temple on Saturday mornings as our cousins. My mother would drop us off at my aunt's house. At their breakfast table we ate toast spread with Cheez Wiz or peanut butter and then walked with our cousins across the street to the modern synagogue with its rectangular multicolored panes of stained glass. By the time Kim was three we had already been confirmed and no longer went to temple. My mother did not send Kim to Hebrew school, for reasons that had to do with the fact that

Kim's father was a gentile, though later she said she regretted it. By the time Kim would have started Hebrew school, my mother's faith had been shaken. Her God had taken away her beloved and, thinking that she could never find another man as good as my father, I believe she married an unbeliever and by Jewish law (the Torah states that the children of such marriages would be lost to Judaism) entered the world of the forsaken.

Last year Lucas prepared for his bar mitzvah. Part of my insistence that he go to Hebrew school concerned my desire to instill in him a sense of faith. He learned his Torah portion with a tutor every Sunday night and attended private meetings with the rabbi. At night before bed he recited his prayers and incantations, and the sound of the ancient language of Hebrew filled the apartment. Some days I would hear him reciting his Haftarah in the shower. On the day he would make his covenant with God he stood at the podium wearing his yarmulke and prayer shawl, leading the congregation filled with his friends, family, grandparents, aunts, uncles, and teachers, his beautiful voice the only sound filling the hollow temple. Surely the joy of God beamed down on him, I thought. Surely he was blessed.

When I was young I liked going to synagogue to listen to the rabbi tell stories from the Torah. As I sat in the synagogue, the sun bursting through the stained glass, singing or responding with the other members of the congregation, I became one with that larger world outside myself. I believed God was watching over me, could sometimes feel his presence fill

my being in the synagogue. That my father had died young
haunted me, and I believed then that it had been for a purpose
I did not quite understand, but listening to the rabbi I was willing to believe it would make me a stronger person.

When the rabbi blessed Lucas, tears filled my eyes. He
instructed Lucas to look around at all of his family and
friends in the congregation. "See all these people around
you. They love you. They will always be there for you," he
said. I thought of Kim, as I do at every family celebration
and gathering, her presence a ghost in the room or at the
table, and wondered whether faith and connection to a community might have gotten her through one more day. In his
study of suicide, Emile Durkheim wrote that the greater the
density of the family the greater the immunity of individuals
to suicide. The more an individual was integrated into social groups—religion, family, community—the less chance
of a suicide. Another more recent study from Columbia
University suggests simple family activities can head off the
emotional isolation that can lead to adolescent suffering and
substance abuse.

In one of the writings Kim kept for her composition
class she considered her lack of faith and regretted that she
was raised neither Catholic like her father nor Jewish like her
mother. Would faith in God or something beyond her have
had an impact? Might it have been a link to a world outside
the self—a connection to a community and shared way of life?
Had she continued college where she was affiliated with a community of like-minded others striving for similar goals, would
that have saved her? Would it have been what kept her in the
here and now? Her writing seemed prophetic.

I have been thinking about God lately. All of the classes I am taking seem to mention religion or God. I just don't know anything about religion and I think it is time that I learned.

I was born to a Jewish mother and a Catholic father. According to the Jewish law, you are born of your mother. That means I am 100% Jewish. My parents were divorced when I was still a baby, and I didn't have contact with my father at all. I was never sent to temple or Sunday School, so I just never learned anything about religion. I can't complain because I remember all of my friends hated to go, they all thought I was so lucky. Now, I feel ignorant, I just don't know the first thing about it.

I go to my history class and we are talking about Creation. Some stuff about seven days that everybody seems to know about except me. In my psychology class we talk about evolution vs. Creation and I don't know which theory I believe, I only know evolution.

I want to learn. I want to learn all different religions. I want to be able to pick what I believe in, if anything at all. I bought a book today, it is called "The Religions of Man," by Huston Smith. It is a study of all the religions in the world. It explains the basics of each religion. Maybe this will help me get started in learning about myself also. What my beliefs are and what is important to me.

I have also signed up to take classes at a place called the Jewish Study Service for Adults. I am hoping that this will help me decide if I believe in God. Now I am very anxious to begin this book and learn. Even if I don't find something that I believe in at least I won't be so ignorant when it comes to what other people believe in. I would really like to understand it all.

But instead Kim looked for immediate sanctuary in the arms of boys. When she was in bed with Alan did she feel the power of God or some kind of spiritual bliss? Maybe because she could not have faith in herself, she turned to the religion of damaged love, the oblivion of smoking dope, the frantic, I-feel-something ecstasy of coke. She was so young.

In trying to understand the psychological complexity that kept Kim locked in Alan's grasp, I read in one of the professional studies that people who have suffered neglect by a parent tend to overvalue sexual satisfaction. They eroticize their dependent longings, and these needs become valued above all others. A father helps a young girl to define her sexuality; his adoration and acceptance allow her to feel desirable and comfortable. If a young girl is deprived of an accepting and loving father, she may become uncomfortable with intimacy, needy and afraid to lose any love she finds, go to the extreme and eroticize her terror of loss.

Since the loved one becomes a part of you, you must not lose him. The thought of loss is frightening, Kim wrote in her diary. *The fear of loss keeps some of the feelings of love inside.*

And because she did not want to face those of us who saw through to the potential of her true self, she hid herself from us and her world grew smaller, sometimes no bigger than the bed she slept in on those nights when she lost her faith.

ZEUS AND HEBE

In thinking about Kim's relationship to her father, I am reminded of the story of Zeus and Hebe. Zeus, the last child born to Cronus and Rhea, was married to Hera. In Greek mythology, his golden throne was on the highest summit of Mt. Olympus, and he was revered by both gods and mortals, but he could be unpredictable. The god of weather, his dark moods caused the earth considerable suffering. Zeus was also known to be susceptible to the power of Eros, or love, a weakness which enraged Hera and for which others paid the price. His youngest daughter, Hebe, goddess of beauty and youth—the patron goddess of young brides and an attendant of the goddess Aphrodite—was his cupbearer. She had the honor of pouring wine for the gods. As she did for her father, she poured wine for all men.

DREAM LIFE WITH KIM

During the months I attend the support group, I begin again to have dreams of Kim. In each dream she is a toddler and possesses the uncanny, open expression of a child not yet troubled by the world, not yet bruised. During the dream I am awash in a peacefulness I've rarely experienced since Kim ended her life—it is so nice to be with her—but upon waking, I feel myself growing almost paralyzed with the dread of having to return to the world where I can no longer speak to her or be in her company. It is not only because of my deep regret and horror (there is no word I know in the English language that can adequately explain this emotion) that she is no longer alive, but because I've come to feel that if Kim could look back on what she did, and its outcome, she'd regret it, too. To suffering adolescents, suicide can feel like an instant cure for their mental anguish and punishing thoughts. They may not fully understand the permanence of death. They may think of it as being in a safe place, like a womb. But they may not understand that they might never awaken.

THE DREAM LIFE OF ANGELS

I go to the video store and am attracted to an obscure film, *The Dream Life of Angels,* which I rent and bring home. The film is about two girlfriends, one blond, the other brunette, who work in a factory and become as close as sisters. One of the friends falls for a cruel and distant lover, and the film follows her self-destructive path. The mood of her days and nights depends on when he will call or see her. She is euphoric when they are together, despairing when he is gone; she believes she can't exist without him. When her lover abandons her, she curls up on her bed in the fetal position. The pain of existence is unbearable. She throws herself out of a window.

No matter how painful, do people end their lives because of a breakup? Or is it simply the triggering event, like getting busted for drugs or being caught cheating at school, that finally allows the individual, no longer able to tolerate feelings of loneliness, hurt, and inadequacy, to enact a form of self-revenge that has been percolating in the mind, perhaps for years? The Italian poet Cesare Pavese, obsessed with suicide for most of his life, never attained a satisfying, sustaining relationship with a woman, though he had many lovers. In one of his diary entries, after the unraveling of a relationship, he wrote: "No one ever kills himself for the love of a woman, but because love—

any love—reveals us in our nakedness, our misery, our vulnerability, our nothingness."

CHECKLIST FOR THE
SURVIVOR OF A SUICIDE

1. Overwork to compensate for the guilt of being a
    survivor.

2. Never waste a moment, as if to prove the purpose of
    your existence each waking hour.

3. Get used to the feeling of shame as if, stamped
    across your chest, is the letter S.

4. Never allow yourself pleasure for too long—this is
    your punishment for being among the living.

5. Observe your child as if under a microscope for
    signs of emotional distress.

6. Question the meaning of existence.

7. Be prepared to get emotional at the announcement
    that your sister's best friend is getting married;
    when you overhear two teenage girls talking on the
    subway; when your twentysomething assistant, who
    reminds you of your sister, tells you her boyfriend
    has broken up with her.

8. Be grateful you married a man like David. Even the
    sturdy sound of his name is comforting.

INTERVENTION

My mother encouraged Kim to see a therapist; we all did. She met with one doctor sporadically—his appointment card was in her wallet at the time of her death—but in the year before she ended her life Kim refused help. In the last two or three years of her life, I tried to convince Kim to move to New York or go away to college, worried about her situation in Cleveland. But she was intractable in her refusal to leave the anchor of home and Cleveland. After she died I couldn't forgive myself for not having tried harder. My therapist suggested that I was powerless to change Kim's inner drama and explained that though siblings often share similar inner worlds, sisters cannot replace the primary relationship a child has with her parents. On one level, this made sense, and yet I didn't believe my therapist, or I wasn't ready to hear it. If I forgave myself, I'd be relinquishing my responsibility.

I recalled the time we tried to get Kim hospitalized, approximately a year before she died, concerned that she seemed increasingly dependent on drinking and getting high—the substances, I imagine now, numbing her body to numb her psychic pain. I read later that self-medication through substance abuse can temporarily relieve inner anguish but also obscure symptoms of depression. Not long before, when I was home for my wedding, I opened the door to her bedroom and was overcome by the smell of bong juice soaked into the carpet and the stench of stale cigarette smoke. I heard her vomiting in the bathroom in the early hours of the morning after she'd come home from a bar, but I said nothing, remembering the days when I was her age. Perhaps by then it was only when she was high that she could find the part of Alan that gave her pleasure, or that she could bear herself.

She stockpiled over-the-counter drugs as a way of self-medicating. On the last night of shivah my sisters and I cleaned her room, afraid our mother wouldn't be up to the task once we returned to our lives outside Cleveland. Kim's top drawer was like a medicine chest, filled with every kind of over-the-counter pill you can imagine. In my reading I learned that emotional or psychological pain almost always manifests in physical symptoms such as headaches and stomachaches.

Cindy, training as a clinical therapist, flew in from California to arrange the details for admitting Kim to Hanna Pavilion, the psychiatric arm of University Hospitals. Later she re-called how painful it was to be training to help others in psychological pain and not to have been able to reach Kim. I had been home for my wedding just a few weeks earlier and was concerned about taking more time away from work. At least that is what I told myself. But in retrospect, I think I was afraid for Kim to see that I was disappointed in her. I thought if Kim sensed my disappointment, it would make her feel I no longer believed in her. Or maybe I was just afraid. After she died, my mind kept circling back to that time. Maybe if I had gone home, too, Kim might not have resisted getting help.

Though Kim agreed to be admitted to the hospital, rec-ognizing she was struggling and needed help, she was anxious about it. We planned the intervention not only to extricate her from the substances we were afraid had or might eventually become addictive but also to distance her from the unhealthy relationship she had developed with Alan and to remove her from the immediate situation of her home life. Al Alvarez describes his life before his suicide attempt as "so cluttered and obstructed that I could hardly breathe. I inhabited a closed, concentrated world, airless and without exits. I doubt if any of this was noticeable socially: I was simply more tense, more nervous than usual, and I drank more. But underneath I was going a bit mad." About the need for respite from even the people we love when we are in psychological pain, one of Virginia Woolf's characters in *Mrs. Dalloway,* her novel that foreshadowed Woolf's own suicide, says, "The people we are most fond of are not good for us when we are ill."

William Styron believes that being hospitalized, as much as he scorned aspects of the therapeutic agenda, like group and art therapy, was the place where he found peace. Days after he checked in his "fantasies of self-destruction" all but disappeared.

> It is something of a paradox that in this austere place with its locked and wired doors and desolate green hallways—ambulances screeching night and day ten floors below—I found the repose, the assuagement of the tempest in my brain, that I was unable to find in my quiet farm house . . . but the hospital also offers the mild, oddly gratifying trauma of sudden stabilization—a transfer out of the too familiar surroundings of home, where all is anxiety and discord, into an orderly and benign detention where one's only duty is to try to get well.

However, once at the hospital, filling out the admissions forms, Kim grew more uncertain. Cindy said that my mother, in an attempt to be supportive, told Kim that she also had a problem with dependence on substances and that it was nothing to be ashamed of; she was proud Kim was seeking help. My guess is that my mother had rarely been medication-free since my father died, subsisting on a combination of prescribed medications: stimulants, Valium, Xanax, antidepressants, and sleeping pills. As she was completing the intake interviews, Kim got scared. "I don't need to be here," she said, kneading her hands as she did when something troubled her, afraid of being thought of as someone who needed professional help. Maybe she missed Alan. "I'll get through this on my own. I'm really okay," Cindy told me she said. And because she was an adult, she could not be admitted without her consent.

THE MEANING OF WORDS

My mother recently told me of the times those last months when Kim came to her in the middle of the night, crying inconsolably. Once she said she wanted to die. "Did you ask her what was wrong?" I asked. "Kimmy would never tell me anything," my mother said. "I could never reach her." When I related this incident to my therapist, she said, "Kim didn't have the words. At her age, only twenty-one, it is very difficult. It takes a lot of persistence to find the words." Kim wrote in her journal in an entry dated 11/4/85:

It's been a long time since I've written. I really shouldn't wait that long. But I just don't know how to write half of the stuff that I want to say. I wish I could write down the way I feel and could express it to other people. I just have so much trouble doing it.

In *Mrs. Dalloway*, Septimus Smith, a veteran of World War I, suffers from recurring hallucinations and eventually commits suicide by jumping out of a window. "Communication is health," the narrator of the novel muses. "Death was defiance. Death was an attempt to communicate; people feeling the impossibility of reaching the centre, which, mystically, evaded them; closeness drew apart; rapture faded, one was alone. There was an embrace in death. But this young man who had killed himself—had he plunged holding his treasure?"

Formulating our own words about our lives translates our interior hieroglyphics into the stories we tell ourselves to make events from our pasts more understandable, give them shape and meaning, organize the chaos of the unconscious where we most often dwell.

THEY GROW TIRED OF BEING A BURDEN

In group the young man with the tattoo of his wife's name on his arm tells his story. His wife ended her life after an episode of postpartum depression when their child was born. He talks about his wife's ambivalence about becoming a mother. After their daughter was born she grew severely depressed, experienced a psychotic break, and was hospitalized. Six weeks later, her depression stabilized by medication, she returned home. The baby by then was living with her brother and his wife. "Once she'd come home everyone thought she'd been getting better," he said. "But she was still tortured about our baby living with her brother and about the burden of her depression. I came home one day from work to find that she'd hung herself. I think she got tired of burdening me," he said. "I wish we'd never had our baby. I don't know how to live without her."

People who end their lives are often tortured by their inability to free themselves of inner demons and by the pain they feel they are causing others. Virginia Woolf, who suffered repeated breakdowns, wrote about her worry of being a burden in her last note to her husband before she put on her overcoat, filled its pockets with stones, then walked into the River Ouse near her home and drowned herself:

> I shan't recover this time. I begin to hear voices, and I can't concentrate. So I am doing what seems the best thing to do. You have given me the greatest possible happiness. You have been in every way all that anyone could be. I don't think two people could have been happier 'til this terrible disease came. I can't fight any longer. I know that I am spoiling your life, that without me you could work. And you will I know. You see I can't even write this properly. I can't read. What I want to say is I owe all the happiness of my life to you. You have been entirely patient with me and incredibly good. I want to say that—everybody knows it. If anybody

could have saved me it would have been you. Everything has gone from me but the certainty of your goodness. I can't go on spoiling your life any longer.

Nathan Kline, a noted scholar on affective disorders and suicide, believes that a person who is depressed is often quite consciously guilty, and what he feels guilty about is being depressed. "He has failed in his own eyes the test of will and spirit. He blames himself for his weakness, and he assumes that others blame him, too." In her journal Kim wrote: *My plan now is to turn mean. Blow-off my friends and family and make everyone hate me. If nobody cared then it would be easy to leave. I'm so trapped.*

THE SUICIDE'S LAST LUNCH

My aunt Harriet told me that she had taken Kim to lunch a few days before she died. I think of the courage it must have taken for Kim, beleaguered by despair, to have kept the date with Aunt Harriet and not cancelled. Perhaps she was privately saying goodbye. Kim and Aunt Harriet used to have lunch together at Stouffer's on Shaker Square, a place where the blue-haired ladies of Cleveland dined and where Aunt Harriet loved to eat. I can imagine what Aunt Harriet ordered: a chicken salad sandwich on white toast and black coffee. Kim probably ordered a hamburger, french fries, and a Coke.

HER FAVORITE FOODS

1. Pizza from Geraci's (Cindy and Laura used to work there as waitresses when Kim was growing up, and like us, she developed a passion for Geraci's famous pizza sauce)

2. Steak and baked potato with sour cream

3. Marvin's Mistake sundae

4. Kraft Macaroni & Cheese

5. Scrambled eggs (sometimes she made herself a plate of eggs after she came home from a night out with her friends)

6. Hamburger and french fries

7. Olivia's silver-dollar pancakes

8. Red licorice

9. M&Ms

Aunt Harriet never had children, and my mother, who lost her own mother early, was her surrogate daughter. We kids were like her grandchildren. Kim was attached to Aunt Harriet, and Aunt Harriet was crazy about her. (After Kim died Aunt Harriet set up a fund in Kim's name at the Cleveland Sight Center, where Aunt Harriet volunteered.) Here is a get-well card Kim wrote to Uncle Joe, Aunt Harriet's husband. At the top of the card, Aunt Harriet dated it "Nov. 1975, age 7":

Dear Uncle Joe,
   My mom's birthday is Dec. 31 and she will be 42. I miss
you so mutch. I wish I cood see you. I'm so sorry that you
brocke your ankle. I like the way you say sleepy when you
say fleepy.
   Love,
   Kim Elizabeth

When Kim came to visit they baked cookies, and Aunt Harriet measured Kim against the wall to see how much she'd grown. Until the day she left her apartment and moved to an assisted-living facility, Aunt Harriet still had the pencil ticks on the wall in her kitchen marking Kim's growth.

> *It's so nice to be happy. It always gives me a good feel-*
> *ing to see other people happy. There are so many ways to*
> *bring joy to people. Bringing joy to others is the best way*
> *to bring joy to yourself . . . just dropping by to say "Hello!"*
> *to my elderly Aunts really makes their day. It makes me*
> *feel good to know that I am loved that much and that im-*
> *portant to them. . . . The smiles I've seen on my Aunts'*
> *faces makes me feel absolutely wonderful. It is so easy to*
> *achieve.*

(journal from composition class, May 3, 1988)

When Aunt Harriet described Kim at their last lunch to-gether, she said that something was wrong with Kim's eyes, a vacancy, as if she wasn't there anymore. Days before Kim died she must have folded up into a place inside herself that she couldn't be pulled back from. It is the only explanation for the kind of terrible courage it takes to end one's life. I'm not sure how long Kim was in that state before she took her life, but from her diaries I suspect it had been going on for a few years. When she was nearing eighteen she wrote in her diary:

> *Well, I'm almost 18 now. I had all these plans & I'm not doing anything that I dreamed about. My Dad said I'd fail at most things, I guess he's right. I'm hopeless. Everybody's leaving soon. I'm planning to go to school in January, but the way I've been feeling I don't think I'll make it.*

After reading those words, of this I am now certain: the suicide leaves a map of her fate long before she dies. Love blinds us to this. We go to sleep. We wake. We pray. We hope. We wait for the leaves to turn a different color. But we rarely expect the worst. Or imagine that when crossing the street and a bus passes by our beloved feels herself wanting to be sucked under. We don't want to think of those we love being in life-threatening pain.

In my reading about why suicidal people become isolated, I learned that people who are hurting emotionally think very little of themselves and act in ways that will cause those they love to think poorly of them. They seem to need to dramatize their inner disdain.

I draw comfort from picturing Kim with Aunt Harriet in the large and hollow room of the restaurant in the last few days before she died, soaking up the love reflected in Aunt Harriet's vivid blue eyes. I can picture Aunt Harriet, dressed in her cashmere sweater and wool pants, reaching for the basket of rolls on the table and offering the bread to Kim. I can picture Kim, her snug stretch jeans tucked into high-heeled cowboy boots, a long plaid work shirt open at the neck, reassuring Aunt Harriet, whom she knew worried about her, that she was going to start school again in the fall and that she was doing fine. Perhaps part of her still wanted to believe it.

THE CRUELEST MONTH

Two days later—who can say why?—Kim found it harder to endure the voices of despair inside her head. She was restless, tired of the handful of books on her shelf, the same four walls with all their familiar demarcations, the unchanged roads she traveled back and forth between work at the restaurant and home, sinking further into loneliness without the energy to take the first steps outside the hole she had unwittingly dug.

It was April. I go over the day again and again, wishing I could change it. The sky still withheld its color after a long, bruising winter where slush lined the streets, salt stuck to the car, and Kim could find no traction. A long winter without the sound of birds or the sight of flowers in the gardens, no cool green lawns to provide a sense of hope. Kim had little appetite. Couldn't sleep. She wanted to hide from everyone. She wished the sky was a blanket she could curl under and that she could exist without objects, needs, people. Even alcohol and drugs lost their power to numb her. That old and familiar feverish unrest returned, the questions of whether she'd ever be beautiful or sexy or smart enough, the anxiety that she may not be able to crawl out from beneath the gloom. Sometimes the usual things that kept her going—plans with her girlfriends, a new outfit, the attention of a guy she liked to flirt with at work—would pull her through. But not this night. From her downstairs bedroom, as she always did, she could hear her mother walking back and forth upstairs. But she did not want to trouble her. The furnace kicked on. The vents spewed hot air. She couldn't breathe. She had met no one new all that winter to open a fresh door. She weakened. A spark of life penetrated the numbness. If only. She broke down and called Alan, who was once like a father figure to her. The person with whom she had placed her hopes and plans. When she dreamed him, he was powerful. Strong. If only she could see him, just this once. Come over, she said. Please. She made her voice soft and sweet, struggling not to let any desperation show. I can't, Kim, he said. I'm seeing someone. And in the pause between his words the world stopped for a second. *The thought of loss is frightening.* No. Not after everything they'd been through. Pain constricted her chest. She could barely breathe or see the hint of light from the moon outside her window. What was she going to do? If she couldn't have Alan, how could she expect to have anyone? How would she get through the night?

DADDY

In *Father Loss*, Elyce Wakerman writes that a girl who has lost her father to abandonment or divorce "ruminates rather than mourns." She forever hopes for a reconciliation. Her father is alive, and if she tries very hard maybe he will come back. But what if he doesn't come back, or what if he rejects her? She may try to secure that love with another male object—a lover. But what happens when that person disappoints her?

In *The Savage God*, Alvarez writes about the relationship between Sylvia Plath and her father, and the effect it had on her suicide. "God knows what wound the death of her father had inflicted on her in her childhood, but over the years this had been transformed into the conviction that to be an adult meant to be a survivor. So, for her, death was a debt to be met once every decade: in order to stay alive as a grown woman, a mother and a poet, she had to pay—in some partial, magical way—with her life." For Plath, the fantasy of death meant a kind of union with her father. For Kim, and here I speculate, perhaps it was unconsciously meant as a way to wake her father up and make him notice her. As Alvarez points out, "Freud's early theory was that suicide is transposed murder, an act of hostility turned away from the object back on to the self."

Daddy

You do not do, you do not do
Any more, black shoe
In which I have lived like a foot
For thirty years, poor and white,
Barely daring to breathe or Achoo.

Daddy, I have had to kill you.
You died before I had time—
Marble-heavy, a bag full of God,
Ghastly statue with one gray toe
Big as a Frisco seal

And a head in the freakish Atlantic
Where it pours bean green over blue
In the waters off beautiful Nauset.

I used to pray to recover you.
Ach, du.

In the German tongue, in the Polish town
Scraped flat by the roller
Of wars, wars, wars.
But the name of the town is common.
My Polack friend

Says there are a dozen or two.
So I never could tell where you
Put your foot, your root,
I never could talk to you.
The tongue stuck in my jaw.

It stuck in a barb wire snare.
Ich, ich, ich, ich,
I could hardly speak.
I thought every German was you.
And the language obscene

An engine, an engine
Chuffing me off like a Jew.
A Jew to Dachau, Auschwitz, Belsen.
I began to talk like a Jew.
I think I may well be a Jew.

The snows of the Tyrol, the clear beer of Vienna
Are not very pure or true.
With my gypsy ancestress and my weird luck
And my Taroc pack and my Taroc pack
I may be a bit of a Jew.

I have always been scared of you,
With your Luftwaffe, your gobbledygoo.
And your neat mustache
And your Aryan eye, bright blue.
Panzer-man, panzer-man, O You—

Not God but a swastika
So black no sky could squeak through.
Every woman adores a Fascist,
The boot in the face, the brute
Brute heart of a brute like you.

You stand at the blackboard, daddy,
In the picture I have of you,
A cleft in your chin instead of your foot
But no less a devil for that, no not
Any less the black man who

Bit my pretty red heart in two.
I was ten when they buried you.
At twenty I tried to die
And get back, back, back to you.
I thought even the bones would do.

But they pulled me out of the sack,
And they stuck me together with glue.
And then I knew what to do.
I made a model of you,
A man in black with a Meinkampf look

And a love of the rack and the screw.
And I said I do, I do.
So daddy, I'm finally through.

The black telephone's off at the root,
The voices just can't worm through.

If I've killed one man, I've killed two—
The vampire who said he was you
And drank my blood for a year,
Seven years, if you want to know.
Daddy, you can lie back now.

There's a stake in your fat black heart
And the villagers never liked you.
They are dancing and stamping on you.
They always knew it was you.
Daddy, daddy, you bastard, I'm through.

SYLVIA PLATH

THE SOUND

I am sitting on the deck of Cindy's house in Connecticut over-looking the sound, drinking a glass of wine on a hot and humid Monday evening in August. "Here's what I feel guilty about," I say. "How I was afraid to really talk to her about her inner pain, which I knew was there but thought would pass. How I wish I had gone home that day when we were trying to get her hospitalized. Do you think it would have made a difference?"

"We are not that powerful. We can't know what might have gotten through to her," Cindy says.

"Do you think that she wanted to be saved? That she understood the finality of her act?" I ask.

"Sometimes I do. And sometimes I don't."

"I think that, too," I say. "And that it was also bad luck. The way everything crashed down on her on that one day. How the stars were not aligned in her favor. Do you think she wanted to die?"

"Perhaps in that moment or those hours."

"Do you think about it?" I ask.

"All the time," Cindy says. "But I think about it in terms of fate and destiny. There is so much we don't know. About life. About who we are. About why some people are more fragile than others. I like to think she is at peace. That's how I try and think about her."

I know how Cindy agonizes over her patients and over the pain many of them suffer. I know when she tells me about one or another patient anonymously that sometimes it is Kim who must sit in the room with her in therapy. As Kim sits in my study with me, at my breakfast table, she's here with us now, I think, here on this hot humid evening when the seagulls are squawking overhead to make themselves known, when all we wish for is that the heat would break.

"It seems so surreal. That she is gone," Cindy says.

"I know."

ABANDONMENT

Martha Reynolds lived in the house directly behind ours. One day she took the shortcut between our yards and asked if I wanted to play. We bounced a rainbow-colored ball between us on my driveway and became fast friends. What wasn't there to like about Martha Reynolds? She had a chiseled face with a button-shaped nose, rosebud lips, dirty-blond straight hair, and skinny matchstick legs. Who knew what other factors drew us together aside from the wake tragedy had left in both of our homes: mine resulting from the sudden loss of my father and hers from the fact that her mother had a stroke, was paralyzed and confined to a wheelchair. What must it have been like for Martha to return home each day after school to her mother in her wheelchair, an ashtray and pack of cigarettes on the tray next to her highball glass of scotch on the rocks? Mrs. Reynolds wore her neck-length hair pinned back from her face on one side with a small colored bow. One of her arms lay weightless on the tray; the other operated the wheelchair. When we came in the door from school she always offered us a snack. In the kitchen we could hear her engraved gold lighter flick as she lit a cigarette. When we retreated up to Martha's bedroom her rambunctious dog jumped on top of us and peed on the rug. In Martha's light blue bedroom we played endless hours of Barbie. Moved our CandyLand markers along the colored road made of gumdrops and licorice. Hoarded our play money. In the summer we hung out in the little playhouse in her backyard where her older brother once pulled down our underpants. But not once did we speak about what it was like to live with a mother who was paralyzed in a wheelchair, or without a father. Questions plagued my girlhood thoughts when I was alone at night in my own bed, frightened by what I did not understand: how did Martha's mother get up the stairs to go to bed? How did she take a bath? Comb her hair?

When we were in the sixth grade Martha's mother had another stroke and died. The halls of our school went quiet. No one said a word. It seemed like a dark curtain had fallen over our childhoods. A few months later her father, who went downtown to work each day and returned home to sit in front of the television, remarried, sold their house, and moved Martha and her brother with him to another suburb forty-five minutes away from Shaker Heights. It was as if he had moved the family to another country. Martha and I lost touch. Then out of the blue, a few years later, Martha invited me to sleep over and my mother drove me to her house. We must have been fourteen or fifteen then, that awkward time when one girl can suddenly hit puberty and look like she is sixteen and another still looks like a little girl. I was surprised at how grown up Martha was when I saw her. How beautiful and shapely she had become. I felt as though I barely knew her.

That night a group of boys came over and we went downstairs to the party room in Martha's basement. One of the boys lit a joint and poured rounds of peppermint schnapps. The next thing I knew, I woke up to find Martha pressed against her boyfriend's chest. Jealousy made my insides ache. My mother picked me up the next day and I waved goodbye from my mother's yellow Comet to Martha, who was standing by the front door of her house. She ran down the driveway and gave me a hug. That was the last time I saw her. I envied her quiet beauty; her long, skinny legs; her perfect, soft face; and her ease around boys. I did not know then that in three years' time she would be found with a bullet in her head, dead by her own hand. Was it a predisposition to suicide that killed her? Mental illness? Or was it abandonment, grief, or dread?

LAST DANCE

In my mind's eye Kim stroked her eyelashes with Long Lasting Mascara and brushed her wavy blond hair to regain its shine.

Dabbed her wrists with musk. Wore her favorite jeans and a sexy black lace top, convinced she might see Alan. But once inside the dimness of the bar, the white strobe light making all the bodies swirl in a neon blizzard of snow, the night must have lost its superficial luster. She must have looked around at all the strangers packed in the place, remembering the night he sought her out and followed her from one crowded room to another. He wasn't there. Not him. Not anyone. Longing consumed her. Maybe someone leaned over the bar to talk to her. Hey, you look cute. Wanna do a line in the bathroom? Tick tock. But when she looked into his eyes, she saw only her own emptiness and the life being lived just outside her grasp: a couple kissing in the dark, friends laughing, moments that on another day, in another place or time, she might have shared. The white lights swirled. Made her dizzy. In the bathroom she looked at herself in the mirror. Her reflection was blank. It was as though her true self had vanished and only a ghost remained.

Sometimes I get a funny feeling in my chest. It's sort of like something is the matter and I can't grasp what.

When she got back home it was late. Past midnight. Everything was as she had left it. Her bedroom with all the familiar objects: dresser, makeup mirror, bulletin board filled with snapshots of friends from a lost, faraway time. Her mother, upstairs in bed, drugged into the long sleep she would not awaken from until well past morning. Father long gone, as if he had forgotten he even had a daughter. Sisters creating lives far from home; tomorrow no different from the shipwreck of the day before, with all those empty days ahead to fill. She took off her clothes, put on her sweatshirt and sweatpants, crawled into bed, but sleep would not come. Her mind crowded her with all the same questions and doubts. She was tired of worrying everyone. She picked up the phone. Perhaps if she could see him she could manage one more night. It's late, Alan, her Prince of Darkness said, perhaps too stoned to hear the depth of despair in her voice. Her mind, thick and cloudy, consumed with inchoate feelings, the color of dull ash. "I'm going to a place far away," she said, tasting remnants of the night's poison on her lips. There I will never have to need him. Or anyone. Perhaps she dreamed, when she put her head on the coolness of the leather car seat, by then so very tired, that he would come and find her.

THE LATE HOURS

There came a moment when she knew that all her hoping, prodding, and pleasing, when, instead of embarking on her own path she'd recommitted to their relationship, when all those days taken up with the struggle of him, being pursued by him, dedicated to him, longing for him (to be near her, inside her, away from her), trying to change him, counsel him, support his drug dealing, cope with his brushes with the law, his possible infidelities were a waste. All those years in which she had made every effort to try to be what he wanted her to be, to do whatever she could for them to stay together, were now meaningless. He ended her struggle, at least for that night, and cut what she had come to see as her lifeline. Though by then she surely hated him, found no pleasure with him—by then pleasure was no longer even expected—she saw she had not the sustenance to be left again. "My grave is like to be my wedding bed."

My only love spring from my only hate!
Too early seen unknown, and known too late!
Prodigious birth of love it is to me
That I must love a loathed enemy.

She had lost herself and did not know how to build herself back up. She was letting everyone down. She could never become what she or everyone expected of her. Even her father had given up on her. He was right. She'd never amount to anything. She knew she could no longer live in her mother's house. It had grown too small. All the familiar plants, antique furniture, even the way the drapes hung depressed her. Grayness descended like a fog and she could no longer see through it or make it lift enough to see even a glimmer from the other side. I can't, Mommy, I can't, I hear her say. Alan had closed the door on her, as her father had. This time it felt as heavy as a vault, and the only door left open—the door back to her childhood house—was too small to go back through. I will go to sleep now. When I awaken it will all be over.

I should have told her I had once loved a boy, too. I was her age. We were young and something happened and it all changed and I knew he would never come back to me. I thought I would not be able to go on living. I thought I'd die of a broken heart. I cried all night and when I got up my eyes were so puffy I could not see. I thought my tears would bring him back to me. How was I to know then that I'd get beyond it? I woke up each morning and thought of him and wondered why he did not call, why he stopped loving me. What was it about me that had turned him away? I should have told her that getting through it is like walking. Put one foot in front of the other, so that each step takes you one step further from the pain. I should have told her that each morning I did not want to get up and face the day and yet each day I did get up, and slowly things began to change. I began to feel better. I should have told her that I knew it didn't seem possible that it would happen but it would. In a while the feeling that makes it seem as if you've lost your other half will slowly vanish and you will see how lucky you were to escape. You were no longer happy. You'll meet someone else. Someone will fall in love with you. You'll have a child. But what I couldn't have known was that the person she thought she could not live without was linked inside her to someone bigger, someone who ruled the world like Zeus, linked to grief as deep as it could get, a primal grief. Daddy, I want to get "back, back, back to you," and so she did the only thing she thought she could do. She snuck out of the house, like a little girl sneaking out to play. She opened the door to our mother's car, slipped in, as if she were only going to sleep the long sleep of a Sleeping Beauty. Maybe she thought she would be kissed awake.

MORNING

When I close my eyes I picture the grayness of morning. How the word spoken aloud means both the beginning and the end. Mourning. A bird in the tree in the backyard just waking up. The grass blades with dew on their sleeves coming to attention. The white house with the dark shutters, as if it had already closed its eyes on the world, whose walls once contained our breaths, our hopes and dreams, stands like a memorial. It is quiet. The sky opens its lid and beckons. And then into the sheer beauty of this quiet, a boy walks up the driveway behind the house where every two weeks he is paid fifty dollars to cut the lawn. He senses something isn't right. Exhaust spins its dizzying toxic fumes out of the small crack left beneath the too-heavy garage door in need of oiling. And behind it he hears a chugging sound, an engine running. When he lifts open the garage door, is the scream in the back of my mind his or hers, or all of ours?

FISH

I have grown more obsessed with the fish inside the glass bowl in our kitchen as each day passes. I make sure the water is not too cloudy. That it's been fed. I have come to love its silvery blue skin. Its fins that look like angel wings. Its quiet presence in our kitchen. I know that eventually it will die. When we go away for the weekend I'm convinced that when we walk in the door the fish will be floating on top of the bowl, and when I come home to find it still clinging to life I am elated. "That fish plays dead but he's not. He sleeps on his side. Floating on the top. Then you touch him and he flips out. He's the craziest fish," David says.

part six

NOTHING IS EVER THE SAME AGAIN

I was sitting in my office, in an open cubicle—I was a part-time editor at a publishing house—when I learned about Kim's death. I was almost four months pregnant, but you know all this by now. In my desk drawer I kept a box of saltine crackers and nibbled on them throughout the day to control the nausea. I was on the phone talking to an author when I heard a beep; another call was trying to come through. It was the office receptionist. David was in the lobby waiting to see me. He never showed up at my office to surprise me. He worked downtown and I was in midtown. I went to the lobby and brought him back to my cubicle. He told me my mother wanted to talk to me. His face looked funny, like he wanted to hold me and run at the same time. Before I could question him, he punched in my mother's number in Cleveland. He had carried the news with him for more than an hour, ever since my mother had called him at his office. She wanted him to be with me when I heard.

David sat in the chair next to my desk and looked at me. There were tears in his eyes. I saw him watch the life go out of my face, as I heard my mother's voice tell me—as matter-of-factly as if telling me my sister had broken up with her boyfriend, or gotten married, or was going to college—that Kim had taken her own life. "Our Kimmy is gone," she said. She wasn't hysterical when she told me. For that moment she spoke calmly and lucidly. She didn't say it with shame or hesitation; she said it as testament. Somehow, my mother, in a state of shock, had gathered the courage to tell all three of her daughters that our sister was dead.

David got my coat and my purse and walked me out of my office and into the lobby. I remember waiting for the elevator, and I thought why, where are we going now, there's no place to go, and then going out into the world, into the midst of traffic, with cars honking and people walking, and my sister was dead. It was on the sidewalk, at Fifth Avenue and 42nd Street, that wrenching sounds I didn't know I could make came out of my body. It was sometime after lunch and David was trying to get me into a cab. It was cold outside. It's often still cold in New York in April, though we expect it not to be, after enduring six or seven months of freezing rain and snow and miserable weather. It's cruel to hope and have your hopes shattered. I looked at David's stricken face and thought, look what I've done. I've led an innocent man through the gates of the ruined.

In the same cab we picked up my sister Laura, who also lived in New York, stopped at home to throw a few things into a bag, and got on a plane to Cleveland. I entered the house where I had grown up and thought, now this house is dead. This house is nothing to me now. Friends and relatives came in and out of the house to pay their respects and, though I spoke to them, it was my shadow self that spoke. I wanted to stop time for as long as possible so that I wouldn't have to be away from my dead sister for even a second. That first night in Cleveland it was raining and storming. It was a violent storm, as if the earth and the heavens were doing battle over who was going to claim Kim's spirit. It thundered loudly and lightning lit up the darkness and rain slashed our windows, and I was up in one of our childhood bedrooms curled against the wall and I was weeping. All night we each wept in our separate rooms, me sometimes in the arms of my husband and sometimes alone in the bathroom where I would go to vomit. At two in the morning I heard my mother downstairs in the kitchen. I went down to find her polishing all the silver in the house, and we held each other for a moment and then she went back to polishing and I went back to bed where I did not sleep. The next morning the day was cold and crisp and the sky was shining bright blue and I thought, heaven won. Heaven has her.

THE SUICIDE'S ESTATE

The contents of Kim's room were the entirety of her estate. She had two twin beds that made the shape of an L and a built-in dresser and two closets with sliding doors. In one drawer was evidence of her fetish for lingerie. (Her favorite colors were pink, purple, blue, white, and black. She loved leopard prints.) In her other drawers were numerous pairs of jeans, bathing suits ranging from bikinis to Speedo one-piece suits, sweatpants, and T-shirts. On top of her dresser, a jewelry box of gold chains, hoop earrings, and mismatched cheap jewelry including a Cleveland Cavaliers pin, a coral-colored garter from my wedding, and two little china pudgy bears that fit together like yin and yang, which now reside in a plastic bag in my lingerie drawer.

The night after Kim's death, my mother came up from the basement, where she had gone to gather the laundry, holding a box of Kim's things in her hands and broke down in tears. "This is all she had," my mother said. "My poor baby had nothing." My mother was crying in mourning for my sister's physical presence, but also for the shame-filled life of want she had provided for her last born.

I went into Kim's bedroom and lay on her bed. It was nearly dark. One of her stuffed animals, a monkey, stared at me with what looked like knowing brown marble eyes. I stayed very still, wanting to feel Kim's presence, and when I looked back at the monkey I thought for a second it winked. That same stuffed monkey, some of the stuffing having come out of its hand so that you can see the wire in his fingers, now resides in my apartment. My mother gave it to Lucas one year when we had gone to Cleveland to visit, and now it has found its way to the white rocker in my bedroom. I like waking up to see that monkey watching me with his impenetrable, cool marble eyes. I'm here, they seem to say. I'm not going anywhere.

THE SACRIFICE

It was the day before her funeral. My sisters, my mother, and I were sitting in the rabbi's chambers where he had called us together to discuss the eulogy for the funeral. It was the same rabbi I had heard every Saturday morning so many years ago, when I sat in the synagogue auditorium with hundreds of other young Jewish kids, as he told us stories from the Hebrew Bible to explain the origins of a particular Jewish law or practice—the story of baby Moses floating in a basket on the Nile among the weeds and rushes; the burning bush; Joseph's robe of many colors. The sound of his voice and the passion of his conviction persuaded me when I was a child. I feel sure that it was those stories that formed my moral center, but it was the story of Abraham and his willingness to sacrifice his son, Isaac, for the sake of God that haunted me. Without explanation God asks Abraham to sacrifice his son, Isaac, and Abraham unquestioningly accepts. Early the next morning Abraham sets out on a three-day journey, prepares the altar, binds Isaac to it, and raises his knife to slay him. But as he is about to begin, an angel of God calls out that Abraham should not raise his hand against the boy or do anything to harm him. Later the 613th commandment formalizes God's wishes: "Do not allow any of your offspring to be offered up to Molech" and "Let no one be found among you who consigns his son or daughter to the fire." I remember wondering how a father could contemplate the sacrifice of his son, why God would allow it, and why God would then intervene. Was Kim's act in part a sacrifice to spare her family from her enduring pain and suffering? And if so, why hadn't God intervened? Had Kim's parents violated the commandment of not consigning their daughter to the fire? And if so, what would be their punishment? A lifetime of grief? I did not want to consign Kim to the here and now, or to Dante's "Woods of the Suicides." Suicide is considered a sin in many religions, including Christianity. In Dante, suicides end up in the Inferno as leaves on trees. If a leaf was pulled off, one's thoughts would be broken out of mercy for the suicide:

And therefore the master said, "If you remove
A little branch from any one of these pieces

Of foliage around us, the thoughts you have
Will also be broken off." I reached my hand
A little in front of me and twisted off

One shoot of a mighty thornbush—and it moaned,
"Why do you break me?" Then after it had grown
Darker with blood, it began again and mourned,

"Why have you torn me? Have you no pity, then?
Once we were men, now we are stumps of wood:
Your hand should show some mercy, though we had been

The souls of serpents.

The rabbi's chamber was dark and gloomy. The walls were painted a burnt orange. I sat on a brown leather sectional couch and looked at my mother and my sisters, also sitting on the couch, and for a second felt the shock of reality. Kim should be with us.

Here was the rabbi who had confirmed and married me. He was a short man with tan, wrinkled skin; brown luminous eyes; and a serious, wise face. He spoke softly, but his tenor was stern and convincing. I knew that according to Jewish law suicide is forbidden, and I felt shame that in the rabbi's eyes, and God's, my sister had committed a sin. But if God had wanted her to live, why hadn't He helped her? If there was a heaven I couldn't bear to think Kim would be excluded because she had violated Jewish law.

It was one of those moments in the life of a rabbi, a man whose counsel is sought to explain the inexplicable, that must have caused him great discomfort. I remember he shook his head and remarked that young deaths are always the deepest tragedy and the hardest to understand and bear. He asked us questions about Kim, as if with our answers he could piece together what had happened. Was she in college? Where did she work? Where was her father? Was she depressed? Had she been getting any help? After he heard each answer he looked down and shook his head, seeming to register in that small gesture how we had failed her.

I remember thinking he had nothing to offer us, and wondered if anyone had any wisdom or comfort to give us. We, the four women in that room, held dark, painful secrets and memories about our family and about Kim's childhood, but we did not understand why Kim had given up her will to live. Everyone else—my sister's friends, relatives, lovers, teachers, acquaintances, admirers, and foes—could speculate, but it seemed to me that only we, her family, held the answers to her fragility. And in this came an ominous sense of responsibility, and we were quiet in the face of it.

In Auden's poem "Funeral Blues" ("Stop all the clocks") the speaker mourns the passing of a beloved and describes the sense of annihilation that loss leaves us with:

> The stars are not wanted now: put out every one;
> Pack up the moon and dismantle the sun;
> Pour away the ocean and sweep up the wood.
> For nothing now can ever come to any good.

A suicide is an assault on the very structure of a family; a family is supposed to protect its own. The sense of failure each survivor feels is blinding and, needless to say, our family has never been the same since.

After we answered the rabbi's well-intentioned questions — after he had asked us about our sister's accomplishments, what she loved and whom she cared for, so that he could prepare her eulogy — he asked if any of us had any questions. My oldest sister Laura spoke up. I don't remember exactly how she phrased her question, but she wanted to know whether Kim's suicide was a reflection of her anger. I didn't see the act as violent. I couldn't fathom that Kim killed herself to lash out or hurt her family. In fact, I felt the opposite. That Kim might have seen her act as one of generosity, or of surrender, wanting peace for herself and her family, and if not to free the family of her burden, then certainly not to hurt us. Kim didn't want her family to suffer or worry about her any longer. On that day the rabbi had no biblical story to tell that would console us in our grief. We left his chambers feeling helpless and even more at sea with what had befallen us than before. None of us could weep, nor embrace, nor comfort one another. Grief, I learned, was private and individual. I later learned that, three years earlier, the rabbi's stepson had thrown himself in front of a moving train.

We grow up feeling we are safe from certain tragedies. Suicide happens to someone else, to other families, not our own. Then, in a matter of hours, life has left one of us and the living are eternally changed. Ironically, though feeling inconsolable from the moment I learned that Kim had died, like a stoic I shed not a tear at her funeral—even though at Jewish funerals it is considered appropriate to display intense emotions so that everyone present feels the depth and pain of the loss. My mother, seeing the coffin, threw herself on it weeping.

On the day of Kim's funeral the sky was a bright, crisp blue as if God had said enough darkness and demanded we reside in light. I looked behind me at all the friends and family who had gathered, all the people whom Kim had known and loved, and who had loved her, and I felt an obligation to restore her dignity. I did not want the fact of her suicide to diminish her. We recited the Twenty-third Psalm with the rabbi and our voices formed a chorus in the bright blue Cleveland sky.

> The Lord is my shepherd; I shall not want. He makes me lie down in green pastures. He leads me beside still waters. He restores my soul. He leads me in right paths for the sake of His name. Even when I walk in the valley of the shadow of death, I shall fear no evil, for You are with me: with rod and staff you comfort me. You have set a table before me in the presence of my enemies; You have anointed my head with oil, my cup overflows. Surely goodness and mercy shall follow me all the days of my life, and I shall dwell in the house of the Lord forever.

I knew that Kim's God was a forgiving God and that He had welcomed her into His house, and I felt her tender and loving spirit that is separate from personality and pain, and I knew the meaning of God's sacrifice of her, that we might all understand that evil and goodness lie side by side and out of human weakness and pain there is consequence.

Jewish law mandates that, at the funeral a tear—in Hebrew, a *kri'a*—be made in the mourner's garment opposite the heart. Representing the sundering that the death has caused in the mourner's life, the *kri'a* is started with a small knife and then is extended a few inches.

After the funeral, flowers, trees, the natural world in which I sought comfort folded into obliquity. Everything was happening too fast; my grief could not keep up with it. I had to store it somewhere, and all these years later I am still doing battle with it. It is a war that doesn't end. Sometimes I think I should be the one dead, and Kim should be having my life. I have to remind myself that I am allowed to be among the living even though one hand holds the hand of the dead. And it is with each word I write, transformed by memory, time, and experience, that I relentlessly try to stitch back together what we have lost as if to make a quilt from which to draw comfort.

DR. S.

How does it feel when everything you've felt in your body and deep in your bones, what you privately raged against because you didn't want it to be true, is all confirmed in searing candor? This is what happened when, a few years after I wrote to

Dr. Shneidman about doing a psychological autopsy for Kim, I finally decided to go to Los Angeles to see him. By this time I had digested much about what I thought had happened to her. Maybe I went to see him to confirm what I already believed. I knew that I wanted to understand more about the suicidal mind and why on that particular night she did the unthinkable. Or maybe I went to him to seek comfort. The nicest part, or rather, the nicest surprise about meeting Dr. S. (as I will call him) is that not only was he one of the most psychologically astute people I'd ever met, he was also warm, kind, opinionated, forthright, and deeply learned in literature. He rekindled my interest in Melville and *Moby-Dick,* and through that novel offered me another way in which to think of the unconscious, the thicket in which our unknowable selves reside, where our undiscovered hidden longings lie.

In Greek mythology the souls of the dead are transported on a ferry across the River Styx by Charon, the ferryman of the underworld. The river separates the living world from that of the dead. The survivors must pay a fee in order for their departed loved ones to cross the river, otherwise the souls of the dead will walk in between the two worlds for a century. I think I went to see Dr. S. because I wanted finally, at least in my own mind, to be able to lay Kim's body to rest.

The night before I left for Los Angeles I flipped through a family photo album, trying to decide which photographs of Kim to bring with me. Lucas, then nine or ten, was practicing his violin in the living room. I loved the clear and melodic sounds of his violin, the rhapsodic pitch and depth his bow made against the strings, as if braiding the sounds of happiness and sadness. When he saw me take down the family album, the one my mother had assembled of Kim and our family after Kim died, he put down his violin and scooted over on the couch beside me. Putting together the album was one of the many ways my mother dealt with her grief. The first Christmas after Kim's suicide we all had our own ways to get through the holiday—I remember overscheduling myself to such an extent that I would not have a free moment to feel or take in the sadness that Kim wasn't with us. My mother barricaded herself in her bedroom for days, forbidding us to enter, claiming she was making us a surprise, and did not come downstairs except for occasional brief trips to the kitchen.

On Christmas morning when I awoke and looked out the window at a fresh coating of snow over the lawn and shrubs, I remembered all the previous Christmas mornings with Kim. My mother came downstairs to the living room with three wrapped boxes in her arms. My sisters and I had gathered on the sofa and were already on our first cup of coffee. Inside each box was a photo album that told the story of our family, a montage of photographs from babyhood until the present, including photographs of Kim from the time she was a baby until her trip to the Caribbean with Alan. It was my mother's way of bringing Kim back for Christmas morning. My mother had a difficult time expressing herself verbally, but she possessed a gift for creating tokens of her affection. She used to wrap our Christmas presents in collages she created from magazine cutouts. When you walk into her living room there is a portrait of Kim on her bookshelf. She is four or five, head down and eyes gazing up, blond hair cut in bangs over her eyes. There are photos of her in every room. My mother's youngest daughter does not die in the once-white house now painted a burnt red, with its shutters and trim light brown.

In one of the photographs taken by a professional photographer when she was a baby, her skin without a single mark or blemish, Kim's face rests in the palm of her hand—a pose too old for a baby. In the photograph it appears as though she is winking. I know what's going on, the expression seems to say. Don't think I don't know. In another she is three or four, dressed in her blue snowsuit, sitting on Santa's knee; in others she is on my lap (I am fifteen) opening a present on Christmas morning, inside a miniature car at an amusement park, or wearing a paper birthday hat at her third birthday party. In another she is an awkward adolescent in leggings and a purple sweatshirt, arms draped around her two best friends. Nothing in the photographs distinguishes her life from any other American girl's.

Looking at the photos, Lucas seemed perplexed, as I was, by how quickly the tide can turn. The mind can be complicated and can play tricks on you, I wanted to say to him that night. It can make you turn against yourself instead of at the people you should be angry with. But that night I remained quiet. He leaned close to me on the couch as we flipped through the photos. I saw his mind turning. "Mom, Kim looks so nice," he said. "I wish I got to meet her."

Years ago when I sent the letter to Dr. S., hoping he could help me reconstruct the psychological events and circumstances that led Kim to end her life, I was not fully aware that over the years when I wrote about Kim, sometimes sideways in poems or in novels, sometimes in these pages, I was creating my own psychological autopsy of her.

But what continued to perplex me was how she arrived at the moment of resignation. She must have thought about ending her life many times. But why on that April night did she not find a reason not to? The grieving process is unpredictable. Weeks, months, and years pass, but time passing is irrelevant. It could have been yesterday.

When I first contacted Dr. S., I was not ready to hear what he might tell me. I had looked at Kim's suicide in many different ways until I resigned myself that each layer of reality existed, that one was not more significant than another. But there were still things I didn't understand: how in the swirl of desperation had she lost hope that the darkness would lift and that the quality of her life would improve? The night she died she no longer possessed the intangible thing we all possess even in our darkest moments that prods us forward.

I spent three days and many hours with Dr. S., a short, pleasant, eighty-five-year-old man who spent most of his life researching, studying, and treating suicidal patients. We talked about Kim specifically, and about his work on suicide; we talked about literature. Sontag, Melville, Plath. The first day I explained Kim's place in our family, told him about my father who died and the landscape of loss Kim was born into, and recounted the details of my mother's marriage to my stepfather. I recounted the sporadic connection Kim had with her father. Dr. S.'s face was compassionate and his voice assertive when he spoke. He said that the villain of the piece was her father—he said the word "villain" as if my life and Kim's were narratives, as if all lives were narratives. Hearing it was like having a bomb go off throughout my body. I'd known it, I'd suspected it, I'd written it different ways again and again, but still I had not fully believed it. Dr. S. explained that, from what I told him, he believed her father resented her being conceived and rejected Kim on her conception. My mother's pregnancy changed her sexual accessibility and he resented it. "He was a man who had difficulty with the nuances of life," Dr. S. said. He explained that, because Kim's father chose not to see her, he taught her inadvertently that she was not worthy. She did not understand him or his actions—why he had left her for all those years and why he repeatedly did little to show his regard for her. It was as if there was nothing she could do to please him or change him. Kim picked up the message "Go away, you are no good," and this was the template from which she perceived herself in the world. What Dr. S. said made sense. I listened intently, trying to balance what he was saying with the little I knew of Kim's father. Because I knew so little about his past or his life after he left us, I am uncertain what would have allowed him to assert such a small role in his daughter's life. Believing that the key to personality resides in childhood, I suspect there must have been a trove of hidden reasons, but his inner life remained a mystery to me. Even after the conversation and its persuasiveness, I still believed there was more to the story.

"What about my mother?" I asked. He explained that my mother was needier than her children. She wanted to be taken care of. She made a good first marriage and the worst thing happened: my father died. "Your father loved you. He died. His death was unrecoverable. Kim's father told her by leaving her that she didn't deserve to live." He explained that Kim internalized his abandonment as "What did I do to chase him away?" "Your mother did what she could," he said.

He told me that no matter what I might have done, I didn't have the authority to prove to Kim that she mattered. He explained that I didn't have the authority because I was not her father figure. "But I could have stopped her. I could have done something," I said. "She had grown to depend on me and I let her down." He looked at me. "Your sister was star-crossed. She was hurt early in life and she wanted it to stop. It's that simple. It's not about spinning the bottle of guilt and seeing where it lands."

MASKED MAN

I have left out one part. At her funeral I saw Kim's father again. He sat in the very back. I think he might have been by himself. I thought for a moment of going to him and saying I was sorry. Sorry for your pain, dear old dad. But then I remembered that he wasn't my dad. He'd been on loan to us for a few years, but the term had long since run out. He looked good. He hadn't aged much. I don't think he ever understood that I had once loved him, too. I suppose there is a distant, inaccessible love in every girl's life. I turned around and there he was, sitting on the white painted funeral chair. The mask was gone, and he was not omnipotent, or powerful, or brave, and the sky above us had not changed colors, and there were real tears in his eyes for his youngest daughter. I don't recall that he spoke to anyone.

Before the funeral, when we were getting dressed, I heard my mother talking on the phone in her bedroom. When I asked who it was after she hung up, she said it was Kim's father. I could tell by the softness in her eyes and the nostalgia in her voice that in the few moments they talked, they had been united in their grief, the bitterness receded, mother and father to their child. "You called him?" I asked. "He's her father, Jill," she snapped back, before crumbling, as if she inferred from my question that I thought she had betrayed Kim. After that, to my knowledge, they never spoke again.

THE MELVILLE ROOM

Dr. S.'s study in his home in Los Angeles, where I went to talk with him about Kim, was filled with books. Pictures of his deceased wife and his four sons hung on the walls of his narrow hallway. He described himself as an iconoclast, a thinker and a questioner. He was also a philosopher, a lover of Mozart and Beethoven, and a Melville scholar. One room in his home he called his Melville room and inside were first editions, art, images of whales, and shadow boxes he created of scenes from *Moby-Dick* that reflected his lifelong obsession with the great American novel. He once did what he called a manual concordance noting each time the word "death" appeared in all of Melville's nine novels.

He described a suicide's state of mind as the "damp, drizzly November of the soul" from the opening lines of *Moby-Dick*. When he contemplated the unconscious he referred to Melville's term, "the lower layer," stating that Melville wrote explicitly about the unconscious in *Moby-Dick* five years before Freud was born. To help me understand, he pointed out a scene in which Ahab is chasing the elusive whale and refers to the "lower layer"—the region of the unconscious where our hurts and desires are not readily visible.

> Hark ye yet again—the little lower layer. All visible objects, man, are but as pasteboard masks. But in each event—

in the living act, the undoubted deed—there, some unknown but still reasoning thing puts forth the mouldings of its features from behind the unreasoning mask.

When I asked him why, on that one night, Kim had lost the will to live, he explained that the suicidal mind becomes truncated and narrow. The technical word is constriction, where life consists of two possibilities: either suicide or some grand solution that isn't going to happen. The mind can't see anything beyond wanting the pain to stop. He explained that the person who takes her life sometimes has the grandiose feeling that the world will end. She feels enormously powerful at that moment, that her world will end, and it's true. It stops in her mind. But did she know it would stop forever? I wondered. I explained to Dr. S. that the night she died, Kim told her boyfriend that she was going far away. And her boyfriend didn't realize what that meant. Then she went into the garage. My mother was home. "Did that mean she had wanted to be saved?" I asked him. It was what I always wondered. "Was there a fantasy of rescue?" "Yes," he said. "It dares the mother. I know you are unconscious and sleeping it off. And I will do this right under your nose. But I wish you were awake and alert and would come out and save me. It isn't a yes or a no," he explained. "It's a complicated drama. In her mother's car. With her mother's gun." "So it was as if it was her mother's gun?" I asked. He looked at me and nodded.

"But what could we have done to have prevented it?" I wanted to know. "We could have shaken your stepfather by the shoulders," he said. "Not likely." He stood up and went to his study and brought back a copy of *Moby-Dick*. "Let me read it to you in Melville's terms. You'll get goosebumps on your arms when you hear this," he said. "'There is no steady unretracing progress in this life; we do not advance through fixed gradations. . . . But once gone through, we trace the round again; and are infants, boys, and men, and Ifs eternally.' In the chapter called 'The Funeral,' they've killed the whale and have brought it to the side of the ship. They've stripped it. They strip the skin, the dermis, and they've taken the blubber and they are going to boil it and they have stripped the whale and now they are going to let it go. The carcass, the great mask of death, floats along. That's pure unadulterated genius, that is Beethoven and Mozart combined. We are captive to the early neuroses which are instilled in us. It raises a horrible question about Kim. If she had survived her twenties, would she have committed suicide at thirty, forty, fifty? Would she hit the same helix? The question is how doomed are we? How set are we in our neurotic vices? On the other hand, if I did not believe in the capacity for change, and improvement, and increased happiness I would be psychopathic to propose psychotherapy."

He described what he sees as two views of the human life course. There is the Shakespearean view of man's life as a series of stages you march through—that is, the seven ages of man in *As You Like It* marked off by decades of life. Dr. S. described this as the linear view. Then there's the Melvillian view he described as fluid, as one big age, as in a helix. He believes our life is a spiral of our neuroses and that we are captive of the early neuroses instilled in us. "If your sister survived her twenties, she might have hit the same helix at thirty, forty, or fifty. It's uncertain at what age certain unresolved losses from childhood come back again. Might your sister have survived her twenties? Possibly," he said. "But she may not have survived her forties without having her psychological needs addressed."

He explained that if he were Kim's therapist, he would have asked her two questions. "Where do you hurt and how can I help?" When he said it, my eyes teared up. It seemed so simple, though of course I knew that it wasn't. I knew through my own work in therapy that it was anything but. He explained that as her therapist he would alleviate the pain by "nibbling at the aches" and by creating an environment of trust. The therapist convinces the individual that the only way he will let her down is if he dies. He becomes a stalwart, totally dependent transference figure. "The work is about developing a verbal and hierarchical exchange," he said. "I would transfer to Kim what her father was really saying and present her with a reinterpretation."

"Do you think she could have gotten through it had she gotten past that moment when she wanted to die and had felt hopeless? If she had maybe found a passion, finished school? If she had gone into therapy?" Those were the questions that had been eating away at me. "A lot of things had to happen," he said. "But I wouldn't be doing the work I do if I didn't think it were possible."

"What should you do if you fear someone is suicidal?" I said.

"Dare to ask," he said.

AFTERLIFE

My mother went to see a psychic after Kim took her life. She was worried about Kim. She was desperate to understand the afterlife. She needed to know that her daughter was at peace. I'm not sure whether my mother had been to a psychic before, but one of her best friends swore by this man, and my mother made a special trip to New York to see him. The psychic told her that in the eternal world Kim was holding a cat and that there was a man with her who was watching over her. The man, my mother inferred, was my own father. My mother had the session with the psychic recorded, and it comforted her. I wish I could say I was a believer.

You're too pragmatic, she tells me. Try and feel your sister, my mother says. I talk to her all the time. She's with me always. I can't tell you how many times I ask for her help. Kimmy used to always help me. She knew how to do everything, my mother says.

QUEEN OF THE DEAD

My mother has never been the same since her daughter's suicide, boarding herself inside our house as if the house had become a shrine to her daughter, as if the walls could contain her pain and sorrow. But like Niobe, queen of the dead, turned to stone by Zeus to spare her pain after her children were murdered, my mother's tears of grief still break through.

LOSING A CHILD

The next month's suicide group meeting was dominated by a couple who recently lost their seventeen-year-old son to suicide. He was a student at a high school for the gifted, had tons of friends; everyone said how special he was. "He shot himself outside on the pavement of a building that looked into our apartment," his mother said, weeping. "It was like he was looking out at us. I keep going to that place where he stood on the pavement, trying to see what he was seeing," she said. "You feel responsible. You feel you should protect your child," his father said, anguish like a map of sorrow engraved on his face. When group ended I turned to the couple and looked them both in the eyes, took their hands, and without looking away or being afraid of their pain I said I was sorry. Sometimes it is all we can do. But it is something. It is not nothing.

CHICKEN LIVERS

A woman in the suicide bereavement group lost her little brother. She can't sleep. In her house she has made a room for him. An altar. A shrine. He was her little baby. "My family is severely dysfunctional," she said. "My parents pitted their children against each other. My brother jumped off a bridge and by the time they found his body it was decomposed. The day I found out he had died there were chicken livers in my refrigerator. I put them in the freezer. For years I could not get rid of them. It was all I had."

GRATITUDE

Every morning when I wake up and pour Lucas a bowl of Cheerios and listen to the sound of his teeth devouring them

I know the privilege of being his mother. Not a day goes by in which I don't recognize how lucky I am to have my beautiful child, my sturdy husband, my remarkable and sustaining life.

THE ETERNAL LIFE OF GRIEF

The most mysterious part of grief is that you think you can will it away. You can refuse to think about it. In one part of your mind you can hold it, but sometimes you must let it go. You often war with it. You grieve for a lifetime because those we love are a part of us even after they have left us, even after they have betrayed us, and our love for them, by taking their life with their own hands. Sometimes for days on end you find yourself crying in the middle of a cab ride, or on the subway, or tearing up when your young son has made you laugh by putting on your high-heeled shoes and walking across the living room floor. Sometimes grief disappears for months at a time and you tell yourself, I'm past this now. And then grief comes to visit again like a long-lost friend. It is mysterious, but never take it for granted. Get to know it as well as you know your best friend.

ROMEO AND JULIET

Five years after Kim's suicide I learned that Alan had taken his own life. I had not seen him since the day of Kim's funeral and then at our house when he came to pay his respects. The news of his suicide filled me with cold and numbing terror. Sometimes people who are unhappy unconsciously find each other, and they believe their unhappiness forms a bond that seals them off from the rest of the world. I wondered if Kim and Alan once had a suicide pact or had talked about it, or whether their self-destructive impulses aligned. I'm certain that Kim's suicide haunted Alan, and the guilt must have been unbearable. I'm certain he never found another girl who loved him the way she did.

"Well, Juliet, I will lie with thee to-night," Romeo says of his Juliet, before he drinks the poison. Perhaps their death wish joined them.

> A glooming peace this morning with it brings;
> The sun, for sorrow, will not show his head.
> Go hence, to have more talk of these sad things;
> Some shall be pardon'd, and some punished:
> For never was a story of more woe
> Than this of Juliet and her Romeo.

ENVELOPES

Aunt Harriet was the family chronicler. She knew the birth and death dates of my great aunts and uncles, grandfathers and grandmothers, wrote down the family stories in a diary, kept scrapbooks of newspaper clippings. No more than a week after my sister died, she assembled the identical contents into four envelopes—one for each of my sisters and one for my mother. When Aunt Harriet died the lawyer who managed her estate found the same envelope locked in her bank vault with the rest of her valuables. A day or two after Kim died, she must have gone to the drugstore to do the photocopying for all of us. I imagine her wearing her blue blazer with the gold buttons and soft cashmere slacks, her hair done up in its signature twist, pearl earrings in her ears. Sometimes I think this is what helps us go on: these objects of a life in a brown envelope preserved and kept safe, these physical artifacts that are emblems of someone's existence. Otherwise, our existence, after we cease to be, lives only in the minds of others.

I have finally opened the envelope. I have reread the obituary we wrote. I have looked at the copy of the poem that is buried with Kim's body, read the letters she wrote to Aunt Harriet and Uncle Joe. Her beautiful little poems. I have read her suicide note.

> *Dear Mom, Dear Family,*
>
> *I am so sorry if I hurt you. I love you all! Very much! I just have to go away. I'm tired of being lonely.*
>
> *I know everyone loved me very much. Please don't feel you could have helped. I am very happy now!*
>
> *All my love, K*

Each time I read it, I am still overcome.

THIRTEEN

We have just come home after a weekend at the beach. I turn on the lights, put my bags down, and go into the kitchen.

"Lucas, don't forget to feed the fish," I call to him. He's already gone into his room, anxious to be rid of us for a few minutes after being in the car with us for more than two hours. "Chill out, Mom," he yells back. "Why are you so obsessed with the fish?" He is thirteen. He will graduate from middle school in June and go to high school in the fall. He has one foot in childhood and one in manhood. He is half indifferent to my world and David's, more concerned with the mysteries that dwell inside himself, the possibilities. I do not envy him the swirl of hormones raking through his body. I do not envy him the few pimples that dwell in the creases on his forehead and around the edges of his nose. The heaviness of his elegant body, not yet fully grown. The anxieties that sometimes keep him up at night. These days he listens to his iPod when he is eating his cereal in the morning. Every chance he gets, he covertly goes into his room to instant message with his friends. He is not indifferent to the girls who size him up when we walk down the street together. When I see him look back it is as though a certain kind of silent music rises from his being to meet their gaze. He is not indifferent to those at school who are bullies, or show-offs, or more confident then he is. I want to protect him. I want to hold my body against his like an invisible shield. Don't be disappointed. Do well in school. Make lots of friends. Be loved. Don't turn against yourself. So many do's and don'ts that if I think about it too much I have to take a deep breath. I tell myself he's strong. Solid. But still I watch him. I will not take my eye off the ball. "Don't worry. The fish isn't dead yet, Mom," he says, finally coming out of his secret cave to tap some flakes into the bowl.

CODA

We are at the beach in Uruguay on a vacation with two other families. At the end of the day we decide to take a stroll on the beach together. We walk along the beige pebbly Uruguayan sand, on the other side of the equator from where we live, the squawking seabirds overhead, the beach empty of others as far as we can see. I listen to the familiar and soothing hum of friends we are traveling with, the chitchat of our young teenagers walking behind us enjoying the time together, away from the pressures of their own social worlds, of academia, of the small quarrels with parents now made insignificant by the foreignness of our locale. The smell of something deep and primordial overpowers the air, and then we see a baby seal with her head tucked into the sand, her black flipper twisted on its side, in an early state of decay, flies around her. I will never forget the stench, nor the sight of the seal with her head lowered and one eye visible. I turn to my friend, who is a doctor. "What do you think happened to the baby seal?" I ask. "Sometimes they get separated from the others," he says, "and can't find their way back."

As we continue along the beach, in the ocean's distance one of us spots what we think is the snout and hump of a whale. We watch it dive into the sea and then come up again with a force so powerful it seems to part the waters. I think about all I still don't know about the mind and suicide, and all I do know, and the responsibility that knowledge carries with it. I think about Ahab on his ship, pacing the quarterdeck, possessed by and obsessed with the white whale; I think of Ishmael, in chapter forty-one, the white whale lurking in the depths, as he attempts to understand his complicated captain and his quest.

How it was that they so aboundingly responded to the old man's ire—by what evil magic their souls were possessed, that at times his hate seemed almost theirs; the White Whale as much their insufferable foe as his; how all this came to be—what the White Whale was to them, or how to their unconscious understandings, also, in some dim, unsuspected way, he might have seemed the gliding great demon of the seas of life—all this to explain, would be to dive deeper than Ishmael can go. The subterranean miner that works in us all, how can one tell whither leads his shaft by the ever shifting, muffled sound of his pick? Who does not feel the irresistible arm drag? . . . For one, I give myself up to the abandonment of the time and the place; but while yet all a-rush to encounter the whale, could see naught in that brute but the deadliest ill.

The children rush into the surf while we stand watch. The mist from the spray of the ocean kisses our face, lips, and neck. The sun reaches across the horizon, and in the distance the whale slides back into the dark blue underwater world of mystery and terror far beyond our grasp.

afterword

In the summer of 2020, at the start of the pandemic, I began working on an essay for *Harper's* magazine that further explored *Moby Dick*, to see what more I could glean about the suicidal mind from Herman Melville's famous novel. After reading the novel again, I saw even more clearly the themes of self-destruction and the quixotic nature of the human mind running through its pages. Ahab is on a quest to avenge the white whale that took his manhood and his leg, but in the end, he is caught in his own harpoon line and drowns. His suffering surpassed his reasoning.

I loved re-reading *Moby-Dick*, this time with more life experience under my belt, and listening to an audio version as I took long walks. Still, I had to ask myself why was I revisiting this subject again, after having devoted so many years to writing and researching *History of a Suicide*? I thought I had closed that chapter. This is the unpredictability of grief over a suicide. Joan Didion in *The Year of Magical Thinking*, the memoir about her husband's sudden death, writes, "Grief, when it comes, is nothing like we expect it to be . . . Grief has no distance. Grief comes in waves, paroxysms, sudden apprehensions that weaken the knees and blind the eyes and obliterate the dailiness of life." What returned me to the subject was the need for more knowledge. I depend on it. I grasp for it. I still believe that there is more to learn about the suicidal mind and that more resources need to be devoted to suicide prevention.

In the ten years since I wrote *History of a Suicide*, there has been a rise in teenage suicide. As Andrew Solomon reported in an eye-opening article in *The New Yorker*, "In 2020, according to the Centers for Disease Control and Prevention, in the United States suicide claimed the lives of more than five hundred children between the ages of ten and fourteen, and of six thousand young adults between fifteen and twenty-four. In the former group, it was the second leading cause of death (behind unintentional injury). This makes it as common a cause of death as car crashes. . . . A recent study published in the *Journal of Affective Disorders* found that about a third of child suicides occur seemingly without warning and without any predictive signs, such as a mental-health diagnosis, though sometimes a retrospective analysis points to signs that were simply missed."*

Suicide is like a death spell, and once it is cast in the mind as an option, it's as if the individual can't get away from it. The desire for pain to cease is so great, it seems it can only be relieved through suicide. Or, if lucky, through intervention. The rub is this: most suicidal individuals struggle on their own and keep their urges private. As a society, we have not done nearly enough to prevent this tragic scourge. For young people, mental healthcare must begin in the home, in schools, and in pediatricians' offices. All children should be repeatedly screened for mental distress and have access to and attention from mental health professionals.

For those of us who experience the loss of suicide, we are forever left in the abyss of grief and bewilderment. I now consider grief a forever thing—because the pain of loss, the memories, they come back when you least expect it. Over time, the loss becomes integrated into the mind and body, but that isn't to say that the acuteness doesn't return. It might arise after hearing or reading about a friend's suicide. Or attending a wedding, as I did recently and was reminded of the many milestones my sister did not have a chance to experience in her own life. Or seeing a film where the character reminds you of the one you have lost, or wishing your loved one could have met your new puppy (my sister adored and had an affinity for dogs as well as cats, and she would have loved our precious Golden puppy, Sophia!).

Suddenly you are seized with reliving the kind of pain the suicidal person had suffered, the hopelessness and futility they felt during the day and perhaps many days, weeks, months leading to death. The worst is how much you miss them. I argue with psychologists and thinkers who say that a certain kind of grief, of not letting go, is pathological. As survivors, we must figure out a way to go forward, but we must not dismiss those who need to hold on. Everyone's path to acceptance is their own.

Over the ten years since *History of a Suicide* was published, I've received hundreds of emails from people who are suffering from losing a loved one to suicide. A parent, a sister, a brother, a best friend, a spouse. These emails usually begin with gratitude for *History of a Suicide*'s insight into the unique grief of suicide loss and into the bewildering mind of the person committing the act. I try to write back with compassion, sorrow, and sympathy. We who have lost a loved one to suicide are a secret society. I am not sure anyone who hasn't experienced this loss can fully comprehend it.

I'm convinced more than ever that the suicidal person wants to live, tries to live, and yet the pain and fog of despair in the mind ultimately become insurmountable. The suicidal person acts, perhaps, according to an inner narrative which no one else can fully comprehend and we must be mindful of the bewilderment and not judge or turn away. Tragedy comes to get us with no warning or regard to our pain and sorrow. We don't always have the best knowledge of our own selves, as much as we feel we might, and we always understand more when looking back than forward. We know bad things will happen that we can't control. We know our life on this planet is limited. None of us can feel responsible for another person's suffering because we often don't know ourselves well enough to be able to articulate our suffering. Sometimes we go so deep there is no way back. Or it seems there is no way back. We don't want to be a burden. We can't be the person we want to be. We can't think of a way out. We want to close our eyes and be gone. We must embrace even the deepest losses in our lives and honor the moments of the dead and redeem them in their full humanity. If they are flawed, then we are flawed. If death takes one of us too quickly, we must celebrate that life, and the life we have in their honor.

—Jill Bialosky, April 16, 2022

* The Mystifying Rise of Child Suicide," Andrew Solomon, https://www
.newyorker.com/magazine/2022/04/11/the-mystifying-rise-of-child-suicide

** https://afsp.orgstory/afsp-issues-statement-urging-screening-for-youth
-suicide-risk

acknowledgments

Sarah Chalfant at the Wylie Agency first believed in my need to write this book and never gave up her fierce faith in it. The exceptional Jin Auh and the staff of the Wylie Agency supported the book in every way. At Atria, Peter Borland was the best editor any writer could want. His sensitive and compassionate editing and big-picture vision were inspiring and uplifting. Hats off to Judith Curr and the amazing staff at Atria. Nancy Palmquist is the most thorough and careful copy editor on the planet. Her clarity and brilliance are evident on every page. Sanda Bragman Lewis listened, counseled, and guided this project at every turn. I owe her a great debt. Many friends and compatriots read drafts, and their good and sensitive readings improved my clarity and sentences. Thank you all: Diane Goodman, Catherine Barnett, Helen Schulman, Dani Shapiro, Willis Barnstone, Eavan Boland, and Bill Clegg. I couldn't have written this book without the support of my family. My sisters, Cindy and Laura, and my mother gave it their blessing. David and Lucas sustained me in every way.

about the author

Jill Bialosky's newest volume of poetry, *Asylum: A Personal, Historical, Natural Inquiry in 103 Lyric Sections*, was a finalist for the National Jewish Book Award. She is the author of five acclaimed collections of poetry, four critically acclaimed novels, including *The Prize*, and most recently, *The Deceptions*, and two memoirs, *Poetry Will Save Your Life* and *New York Times* bestselling memoir *History of a Suicide: My Sister's Unfinished Life*. Her poems and essays have appeared in the *New Yorker*, the *Atlantic Monthly*, *Harper's*, *O Magazine*, the *Kenyon Review*, *Harvard Review*, *Paris Review* and *Best American Poetry* among others. She co-edited with Helen Schulman the anthology, *Wanting a Child*. She is an Executive Editor and Vice President at W. W. Norton & Company. In 2014 she was honored by the Poetry Society of America for her distinguished contribution to poetry.

notes

ix Jill Bialosky, "A Sister's Story," in *The End of Desire* (New York: Alfred A. Knopf, 1997), 19.

xix T. S. Eliot, "Burnt Norton," in *Four Quartets* (New York: Harcourt, Brace, 1943, 1971), 14.

xxi Herman Melville, *Moby-Dick; or The Whale* (New York: The Modern Library, 2000), 4.

xxii Ibid., 119.

xxiii Emily Dickinson, "Hope Is the Thing with Feathers," in *The Complete Poems of Emily Dickinson* (Boston: Little Brown, 1924), 254.

1 epigraph: Sylvia Plath, *The Bell Jar* (New York: Harpers, 1967), 237.

13, 14 Jean-Jacques Rousseau, *Julie, or the New Heloise: Letters of Two Lovers Who Live in a Small Town at the Foot of the Alps*, translated and annotated by Philip Stewart and Jean Vache (Hanover, NH: University Press of New England, 1997), 311, 319.

16 T. S. Eliot, *The Wasteland* (New York: Harcourt, Brace, 1930), 29.

16 Suicide rates in April: George Howe Colt, *November of the Soul: The Enigma of Suicide* (New York: Scribner, 1991), 249.

16 privately saying goodbye: Edwin S. Shneidman, *The Suicidal Mind* (New York: Oxford University Press, 1996), 52.

18 Al Alvarez, *The Savage God* (New York: W. W. Norton, 1971), 26.

19 "clenching and constricting": Karen v. Kukil, ed., *The Unabridged Journals of Sylvia Plath, 1950–1962*, transcribed from the original manuscript at Smith College (New York: Anchor Books, 2000), 395.

19 Wallace Stevens, "The Snow Man," in *Collected Poems of Wallace Stevens* (New York: Vintage Book Edition, 1931), 9.

22 primates who have lost their babies: Natalie Angier, "Do Animals Grieve Over Death Like We do?" *New York Times* (September 2, 2008). www.nytimes.com/2008/09/02/health/02iht-02angi. 15827535.html, accessed 9/13/10.

23 "the ungraspable phantoms of life": Melville, *Moby-Dick*, 4.

24 "What might have been and what has been": Eliot, "Burnt Norton," 13.

31 Richard Holmes, "The Fantoms of Théophile Gautier," *New York Review of Books* LV, no. 13 (9/14/2008): 63.

60 Bialosky, "The Runaway," in *The End of Desire*, 70.

63 "Sisters," in ibid., 22.

77 John Donne, "Meditation XVII," in *The Works of John Donne*, vol. III, Henry Alford, ed. (London: John W. Parker, 1839), 574–75.

81 effect of the combination of the two drugs: U.S. Department of Justice, Drug Enforcement Administration, Office of Diversion Control, Drugs and Chemicals of Concern, September 2007. www.deadiversion.usdoj.gov/drugs_concern/benzo_1.htm, accessed 9/13/10.

82 substance abuse can decrease one's judgment: Lili Frank Garfinkel and Andrew E. Slaby, *No One Saw My Pain: Why Teens Kill Themselves* (New York: W. W. Norton, 1996), 85.

83 Shneidman, *The Suicidal Mind*, 4.

83 people who are acutely suicidal: William Dickie, "Edwin Shneidman, Authority on Suicide, Dies at 91," *New York Times,* May 21, 2009.

84 suicide is the result of an interior dialogue: Shneidman, *The Suicidal Mind*, 15.

84 "psychache": Shneidman, *The Suicidal Mind*, 13.

88   "whether 'tis nobler": William Shakespeare, *Hamlet,* in *The Riverside Shakespeare,* G. Blakemore Evans, ed. (Boston: Houghton Mifflin Company, 1974), 3.1.59–62. References are to act, scene, and line.

88   "*Romeo and Juliet* to be a study on the impulsivity of teenage suicide": Stanton Peele Addiction website, November 1, 2008. This blog post also appeared on Stanton's Addiction in Society blog at PsychologyToday.com www.peele.net/blog/081101 .html, accessed 9/13/10.

88   "my grave is like to be my wedding bed": *Romeo and Juliet,* 1.5.134.

89   John Donne, *Biathanatos,* Ernest W. Sullivan, ed. (Newark: University of Delaware Press, 1984).

89   Eliot, *The Wasteland,* 29.

90   Eliot, "East Cocker," 29.

90   Eliot, *The Wasteland,* 29–30.

92   Charlotte Mew, "The Quiet House," in *Selected Poems,* Eavan Boland, ed. (London: Carcanet, 2008), 9–10.

96   Lucille Clifton, "the light that came to lucille clifton," in *Good woman: poems and a memoir 1969–1980* (Rochester, NY: Boa Editions, 1987), 209.

98   Thomas Travisano, ed., with Saskia Hamilton, *Words in Air: The Complete Correspondence Between Elizabeth Bishop and Robert Lowell* (New York, Farrar, Straus, 2008), 752.

99   Dickinson, "Shame is the shawl of Pink," in *The Complete Poems of Emily Dickinson,* 1412.

100   Joan Didion, *The Year of Magical Thinking* (New York: Vintage, 2005), 23.

100   "is often overcome by the very obstacles . . ." http://www .encyclopedia.com/literature-and-arts/language-linguistics -and-literary-terms/literature-general/tragedy

110   "To have a parent who is missing": Elyce Wakerman, *Father Loss: Daughters Discuss the Man that Got Away* (New York: Henry Holt, 1984), 4.

110   "Full fathom five thy father lies": *The Tempest,* 1.2.400–405.

110   Sylvia Plath, "Full Fathom Five," in *The Collected Poems*, Ted Hughes, ed. (New York: Harper & Row, 1981), 92.

113   "Moonrise," in ibid., 98.

115   "Tulips," in ibid., 160.

119   Columbia University program to screen suicides: Kay Redfield Jameson, *Night Falls Fast: Understanding Suicide* (New York: Vintage, 1990), 275.

127   "Now old desire doeth in his death-bed lie": *Romeo and Juliet*, 2.1.1–14.

129   Bialosky, "Ruined Secret," in *The End of Desire*, 32.

138   perfectionism is a common thread: Garfinkel and Slaby, *No One Saw My Pain*, 50.

138   "my thoughts be bloody": *Hamlet*, 4.4.66.

138   the opposite of the stereotypical rebellious youth: Richard O'Connor, *Teen Suicide*, http://www.focusas.com/Suicide.html. *Undoing Depression: What Therapy Doesn't Teach You and Medication Can't Give You.*

139   Paul Mariani, *The Broken Tower: The Life of Hart Crane* (New York: W. W. Norton, 1999), 413.

139   "embryonic darkness": Eric H. Erickson, *Young Man Luther: A Study in Psychoanalysis and History* (New York: W. W. Norton, 1993), 24.

142   suicide attempts are failed suicides: Garfinkel and Slaby, *No One Saw My Pain*, 7.

142   about one third of people who attempt suicide: http://health.nytimes.com/health/guides/disease/suicide-and-suicidal-behavior/overview.html, accessed 10/27/10.

144   study of genetic link that doubles carriers' risk of suicide: Greg Basky, "Suicide Linked to Serotonin Gene," *Canadian Medical Association Journal* 162, no. 2 (May 2, 2000), http://ecmaj.com/cgi/content/full/162/9/1343-a, accessed 9/15/10.

144   Swedish study: Bo Runeson and Marie Åsberg, "Family History of Suicide Among Suicide Victims," *American Journal of Psychiatry* 160 (August 2003): 1525–26. http://ajp.psychiatryonline.org/cgi/content/abstract/160/8/1525, accessed 9/15/10.

144 Bakish study: L. Du, D. Bakish, Y. D. Lapierre, A. V. Ravindran, P. D. Hrdina, "Association of Polymorphism of Serotonin 2A Receptor Gene with Suicidal Ideation in Major Depressive Disorder," *American Journal of Medical Genetics* 96, no. 1 (February 7, 2000): 56–60. I received more detailed information about Bakish's work through an email correspondence, and some of the quoted material is from our dialogue.

145 90 percent of completed suicides of all ages: Colt, *November of the* Soul, 41.

146 15 percent of depressed people will commit suicide: Agency for Healthcare Research and Quality, "National Healthcare Quality Report" (2003). This is a widely quoted statistic, though some experts—such as Christopher L Summerville, executive director of the Manitoba Schizophrenia Society—have cited higher figures. See also Bob Murray and Alicia Fortinberry, "Depression Facts and Stats," Uplift Program, updated January 15, 2005, www.upliftprogram.com/depression_stats .html#11, accessed 9/13/10.

146 Shneidman, quoted in Colt, *November of the Soul*, 197.

146 Jamison, *Night Falls Fast.*

146 "still unrest": John Keats, "Bright Star," in Stephen Greenblatt et al., eds. *The Norton Anthology of English Literature, Volume 2*, 8th ed. (New York: W. W. Norton, 2000), 898.

149 "beautiful tyrant": *Romeo and Juliet*, 3.1.75.

153 *Diagnostic and Statistical Manual of Mental Disorders-IV (DSM-IV)*, American Psychiatric Publishing, Inc., 4th ed., June 2000, 24.

154 Samuel Klagsburn, quoted in Colt, *November of the Soul*, 43.

159 "complicated" grief: http://www.mayoclinic.com/health/complicated-grief/PS01023.

163 "enmeshment": Mahler, Pine, and Bergman, "Boundary Dissolution: Dimensions of Boundary Dissolution Gender, Theory, Family, and Development," http://family.jrank.org/pages/172/Boundary-Dissolution-Dimensions-Boundary-Dissolution.html, accessed 9/13/10.

164   Anna Freud quote: Leon Lytryn, M.D. and Donald McKnew, M.D., *Growing Up Sad, Childhood Depression and Its Treatments* (New York, London: W. W. Norton & Company, 1998), 82.

166   suicide wish: Stefan Kanfer, review of *Damned Gifts, Manic Power: Robert Lowell and His Circle* by Jeffrey Meyers, *Time* (November 23, 1987).

166   Robert Lowell, "Symptoms," in *Collected Poems* edited by Frank Bidart and David Gewanter (New York: Farrar, Straus, 2003), 648.

167   Adam Phillips, "First Hates," *On Ticking, Kissing, and Being Bored: Psychoanalytical Essays on the Unexamined Life* (Cambridge, MA: Harvard University Press, 1994), 17.

168   William Styron, *Darkness Visible: A Memoir of Madness* (New York: Vintage, 1990), 34–40.

168   incomplete mourning: Ibid., 81.

169   flowering into madness: Ibid., 78.

169   Kushner's book on suicide: Ibid., 80.

169   parents unaware of 90 percent of suicide attempts: www.pbs.org/wnet/cryforhelp/episodes/resources/sobering-statistics/12/, accessed 9/13/10.

169   Garfinkel and Slaby, *No One Saw My Pain*, 9.

169–170   Alan Wheelis, *The Way We Are* (New York: W. W. Norton 2006), 16.

170   "why the deed was done": Max Malikow, ed., *Suicidal Thoughts: Essays on Self-Determined Death* (New York: Hamilton Books, 2009), 56.

170   for every teenage suicide, there are hundreds of depressed teenagers: Colt, *November of the Soul*, 43.

171   study on hopelessness: Aaron T. Beck, Gary Brown, Robert J. Berchick, Bonnie L. Stewart, and Robert A. Steer, "Ultimate Suicide: A Replication With Psychiatric Outpatients," *American Journal of Psychiatry* 147 (1990): 190–95, http://focus.psychiatryonline.org/cgi/content/abstract/4/2/291, accessed 9/15/10.

171   they do not have more problems: Apter, *The Myth of Maturity*, 248.

171   people are able to tolerate depression: Jamison, *Night Falls Fast*, 94.

171   on hopelessness: Styron, *Darkness Visible*, 62.

171   hopeless, a feeling that conditions will not improve: Suicide Prevention, Awareness, and Support, Suicide.org., www.suicide.org /hopelessness-a-dangerous-warning-sign.html, accessed 9/13/10.

172   people who seem habitually helpless: email correspondence with Dr. George Makari, director and associate professor at Weill Cornell Medical College and author of *Revolution in Mind: The Creation of Psychoanalysis*.

172   Lanny Berman, quoted in Benedict Carey, "Making Sense of the Great Suicide Debate," *New York Times*, February 10, 2008.

175   E. M. Forster, *Aspects of the Novel* (San Diego: Harvest, 1927), 63.

177   Medea: Edith Hamilton, *Mythology* (Boston: Little, Brown, 1942, 1969), 170–78.

181   the Torah says children of such marriages: Deuteronomy 7:3–4.

182   Emile Durkheim, *Suicide: A Study in Sociology* (New York: Free Press, 1951), 14.

182   Columbia University study: www.pbs.org/wnet/cryforhelp/ episodes/resources/sobering-statistics/12/, accessed 9/13/10.

185   Zeus and Hebe: Hamilton, *Mythology*, 39.

186   suicide can feel like an instant cure: Colt, *November of the Soul*, 49.

187   "No one ever kills himself for the love of a woman," Cesare Pavese, *The Burning Brand: Diaries 1935–1950*, entry for March 25, 1950 (New York: Walker, 1952, 1961).

188   self-medication: Garfinkel and Slaby, *No One Saw My Pain*, 85.

190   Alvarez, *The Savage God*, 257.

190   Virginia Woolf, *Mrs. Dalloway* (San Diego: Harcourt, Brace, 2002), 147.

190   Styron, *Darkness Visible*, 68, 70.

192   "Communication is health": Woolf, *Mrs. Dalloway*, 184.

193 River Ouse: Phyllis Rose, *Woman of Letters: A Life of Virginia Woolf* (New York: Harcourt, Brace, 1987), 243.

194 "He has failed in his own eyes": Nathan Kline, Leon Cytryn, and Donald McKnew, *Growing Up Sad: Childhood Depression and Its Treatment* (New York: W. W. Norton, 1998), 72.

197 hurting emotionally: Garfinkel and Slaby, *No One Saw My Pain*, 5.

199 Wakerman, *Father Loss*, 95.

200 Alvarez, *The Savage God*, 35.

200 Freud's early theory: Ibid., 67.

200 Plath, "Daddy," in *The Collected Poems*, 000.

208 "My grave is like to be my wedding bed": *Romeo and Juliet*, 1.5.134.

209 "My only love spring from my only hate!": Ibid., 1.5.138–41.

217 "offspring to be offered up to Molech": Leviticus 18:21.

217 "consigns his son or daughter to the fire": Deuteronomy 18:10.

218 Dante Alighieri, Canto XIII, The Wood of Suicides, *The Inferno of Dante*, Robert Pinsky, trans. (New York: Farrar, Straus, 1995), 000.

219 W. H. Auden, "Funeral Blues," in *Selected Poems of Auden* (New York: Vintage, 1976, 1991), 000.

221 Psalm 23: Liturgy Committee of the Central Conference of American Rabbis, *Gates of Repentance: The New Union Prayerbook for the Day of Awe* (New York: Central Conference of American Rabbis, 1978).

222 *Kri'a*: Rabbi Joseph Telushkin, *Jewish Literacy: The Most Important Things to Know About the Jewish Religion, Its People, and Its History*, revised ed. (New York: William Morrow, 2009), 629.

229 "Hark ye yet again": Melville, *Moby-Dick*, 236.

231 "There is no steady, unretracing progress": Ibid., 704.

236 "A glooming peace this morning with it brings": *Romeo and Juliet*, 5.3.305–9.

240 Melville, *Moby-Dick*, 271.

Permissions